Expedition Field Techniques
SMALL MAMMALS
(excluding bats)

by Adrian Barnett and John Dutton

Geography Outdoors:
the centre supporting field research, exploration and outdoor learning
Royal Geographical Society with IBG
1 Kensington Gore
London SW7 2AR

Tel +44 (0)171 591 3030 Fax +44 (0)171 591 3031
Email go@rgs.org   Website www.rgs.org/go

2nd Edition, January 1995
ISBN 978-0-907649-68-7

Recommended citation: Barnett, A. & Dutton, J. (1995). *Expedition Field Techniques: Small Mammals (excluding bats)*. Expedition Advisory Centre, London, England.

Expedition Field Techniques
SMALL MAMMALS (excluding bats)

CONTENTS

Acknowledgements
About the Authors
Preface

Acknowledgements

Lots of people have helped with this handbook - many in the indirect ways of sharing fieldwork, others by sharing experiences. There are too many to list, but Phil Atkinson, Malcolm Coe, Judith Coffin, Gordon Corbet, Alexia da Cunha, Philip Donlan, Chris Elphick, Fif Robinson and Jon Wright deserve special mention. Very special "thank you's" to Madeleine Prangley and Joanne Dutton. The Royal Geographical Society has provided funds and encouragement for the expeditions on which much of this handbook's field experience was gained. We should also like to acknowledge the staff of the Mammal Section, Natural History Museum, South Kensington for their kindness and patience over many years, and thank the staff of the General and Zoology libraries for all their help. The staff at the Expedition Advisory Centre have been very patient while we have prepared this second edition. Thanks also to Brian Cresswell (Biotrack), Lee Flint (Selfset Ltd), Andrew Ford (Thomas's Europe), John French (Mariner Radar), Hawkins and Manwaring, Anne Hewitt (H.W. Peel & Compant Ltd.), JSP Ltd. and Ray Pitts (RS Biotech) for providing information, advice and products. Madeleine Prangley and Karen Barnett did the line drawings.

This book is dedicated to Jessica, who was born on the 17th November 1994, while this book was being written.

About the authors

Adrian Barnett has worked in the Andes, Amazon, Africa and South East Asia on ecology and conservation projects. His fieldwork has concentrated on mammals of high altitude tropical habitats and rainforests. He read Zoology at Oxford and did his Masters in ecology at University of Wales, Bangor. Formerly, senior research officer on Friends of the Earth's tropical rainforest campaign.

John Dutton has an HND in Conservation Management from Farnborough College of Technology and a BSc (Hons) in Ecology from the University of East Anglia. He is currently writing his MPhil/Phd thesis on the relationship between rabbits and sand dune vegetation on Jersey. Over the last nine years he has given advice on logistics, research and equipment to numerous expedition teams and participated in several expeditions, leading the UEA São Tomé expedition.

Both authors are Fellows of the Royal Geographical Society.

Preface

This book aims to give an overview of the techniques of small mammals study which are suitable for expedition use. It's compass is not exhaustive and many things have been deliberately omitted as unsuitable for the type of field surveys normally undertaken by expeditions. It is above all a practical guide and does not deal with the abundant literature relating to the more theoretical aspects of mammalogy (e.g. socio-biology and population ecology). It's focus is towards surveys and the contribution that these can make to conservation, land management and basic and applied ecology.

We hope that by writing this manual more expeditions will invest the effort required in preparatory work which culminates in fieldwork whose results are of publishable quality. Copies of any such publications would be welcome by the authors and the EAC.

Expeditioners are, by and large an innovative lot and new field techniques are devised on many expeditions. But we need to hear about them to incorporate them into future editions of this manual. So if you have a good idea please send to us care of the EAC - things won't get better without you.

Adrian Barnett and John Dutton
Norwich, November 1994

Section One
SMALL MAMMALS AND EXPEDITIONS

1.1 Introduction

Small mammals do not exist as a zoological group. The term is generally considered to apply to any non-flying mammal weighing less than 1kg when adult. Though there are a few ungulate small deer (e.g. water chevrotian, *Hyemoschus aquaticus*, and mouse deer, *Tragulus* spp.) that are smaller than some of the larger rodents, and quite a lot of the Mustelids (e.g. ferrets, weasels) are diminutive, in practice the term is generally restricted to rodents, marsupials, insectivores and elephant shrews. There are around 1814 rodents, 280 marsupials, 384 insectivores and 15 elephant shrew (Nowak, 1991a,b). The respective percentages under 1kg are around 83.13%, 70.35%, 99%, and 100% putting the total number of non-flying small mammals at around 2104. There are some 4434 species of mammal, of which 3329 are non-flying terrestrial (calculated from Nowak, 1991a,b). This means that, collectively (with bats excluded), there are more small mammals than any other type of terrestrial mammal (63.2%) and constitute nearly half of all mammals (47.45%). It is this group with which this publication is concerned. The focus of this concern is how to study their ecology in the field under expedition conditions. Those who are interested in bats are referred to Mitchell-Jones (1987), which outlines field techniques for bat workers.

A small mammal survey is often included in an expedition's field work plan since:

- small mammals are often quite abundant
- they are comparatively easy to study
- general principles of small mammals ecology are quite well known
- they can be good ecological indicators
- they often exhibit habitat or dietary specificity
- live animals are rarely directly dangerous
- specimens are easily prepared and transported

However, fieldwork studies should not be chosen because they are easy, but because they are useful. Small mammal ecology also has its downsides:

- the literature focuses disproportionately on temperate species
- many areas are very poorly known
- the taxonomy of many groups is poorly worked out

- population densities can vary widely from year to year and from place to place
- not all species are equally abundant

1.2 What types of projects can an expedition do?

There is no point in being too ambitious. Simple basic, natural history-type fieldwork is often very useful. Don't worry, it hasn't all been done before. For many regions valuable contributions can be made simply by collecting data on:

- which species are in the region (Duckworth *et al.*, 1993)
- what habitat(s) they occur in
- altitudinal ranges of species
- reproductive condition of the animals at the time of capture (Henry, 1994; Taylor *et al.*, 1990))
- relative abundance of various species (Feldhammer *et al.*, 1993)
- diet (Canova & Fasola, 1993)
- niche dimensions of: single species (Ligtvoet & van Wijngaarden, 1994; Yom-Tov, 1993), species pairs (Rogovin, 1992) and of communities (Price & Brown, 1983; and papers in Fox & Powell, 1985)
- conservation work needs data on species diversity (Haila & Kouki, 1994), and it is important that its variation be assessed both in time (Henttonen *et al.*, 1992; Martinsson *et al.*, 1993) and space (Lomolino, 1994)
- studies of the limiting factors and natural history of rare and geographically circumscribed species (Snyder & Linhart, 1994)[though caution should prevail when studying them, don't let your study add to their problems]

For groups with special interests or experience, or simply more time, field work can include:

- studies of marked animals (home range, density)
- parasitological studies
- population fluctuations
- assessments of impacts of changes in land use including: effects of grazing (Douglass *et al.*, 1992; Grant *et al.*, 1982; Philips, 1936); effects of urbanisation (Dickman & Doncaster, 1987, 1989); colonisation in secondary habitats (Dwyer, 1984; van Horn, 1982); effects of mines and pollution (Kataev *et al.*, 1994); habitat fragmentation (Adler, 1994; Geuse *et al.*, 1985; Pelikan, 1989; Robinson *et al.*, 1992)
- diet
- predator/prey relationships

- geographical variation in size (Hayes & Richmond, 1993; Norton, 1986)
- aiding systematic work (using non-terminal tissue sampling)(Hogan *et al.*, 1993; Wójcik, 1993; Zanchin *et al.*, 1992)

Take advantage of any opportunities to study or report on phenomena. This category includes:

- observation of predation (Baxter, 1993; Richards 1986)
- dental anomalies (Feldhammer & Stober, 1993; Kompanje & de Vries, 1992)
- unusual colour forms
- effects of natural disasters - e.g. floods, volcanic activity or fires (Christian, 1977; Sgardelis & Margalis, 1992)

Remember, much of the distribution of a species (especially in the tropics) is uncertain (e.g. Tchernov, 1992), and there is always the chance that you will record range extensions (Aitken, 1977a; Chandraseikar-Rao & Musser, 1993; Ochoa *et al.*, 1993; Osbourne & Preece, 1987; Pearson & Robinson, 1990; Ziegler, 1984). Even negative data can be useful in this context (e.g. Dowsett, 1993).

Between 1991 and 1993 around 27 new species of small mammal have been discovered (6 rodents, 2 insectivores and 8 marsupials). The 1994 University of Aberdeen expedition to Madagascar found 3 previously unidentified tenrec species (Wells *et al.*, 1994) Therefore, the chances of you discovering a new species are not as remote as you might think (e.g. Aslin, 1976; Emmons, 1993; Gardner & Romo, 1993; Leo & Gardner, 1993), and their discovery does not always require a great deal of fieldwork (see Scheffer & Dalquest, 1942). Significant discoveries can still be made even in areas whose mammal fauna appears well known (Smolen *et al.*, 1993). It may also be possible to re-discover species thought no longer to survive in an area (e.g. Aitken, 1977b).

Your time in the field is valuable, so don't waste it on inappropriate projects. Elegant manipulative experimental approaches (e.g. Cittandino *et al.*, 1994; Ylönen, 1990) to the study of ecological interactions are generally unlikely to succeed due to limitations of time and resources. Radio-tracking is not for the novice or those with limited time. Behavioural observation and detailed studies of burrowing or arboreal species are also likely to be beyond the scope of a small, short expedition.

1.3 Things you probably cannot do

Time constraints mean that you will probably not be able to study complex, multi-faceted ecological interactions (e.g. Crawford & Seely, 1994; Devenport & Devenport, 1994; Gorman *et al.*, 1993; Jedrzejewski *et al.*, 1992; Kam & Degen, 1994; Michener, 1993), do studies on captive animals (e.g. multi-species behavioural interactions: Kozakiewicz & Boniecki, 1994; activity patterns: O'Reilly *et al.*, 1986; and food preferences: Emamdie & Warren, 1993, or undertake studies of social biology and reproduction: Boonstra *et al.*, 1993; Gliwicz, 1993; Grandjon & Duplantier, 1993; Ostfeld & Heske, 1993; Pugh *et al.*, 1993).

1.4 Preparatory work

There is no point expecting to arrive at your study site, bung down a few traps, get a few rats, do something ecological with them, and then get some brilliant results at the end of it. Pre-field work is required. That it is fundamental to success of the expedition cannot be stressed to strongly. Organise your preparatory work so that you have a back-up project if the main one fails (for whatever reason). Do not get tunnel vision. An example is the 1990 UEA São Tomé expedition when the mammal team collected information on marine and freshwater turtles when their trapping programme met with little success (Atkinson *et al.*, 1994).

Essential preparatory work consists of:

- knowing what species to expect - check the literature thoroughly (Section 15 suggests where to start), and look through the museum collections to familiarise yourself with the appearance of the animals. It is a good idea to make a photographic collection of specimens. This helps in the field and may be useful if you intend using local knowledge. Make a field key, using external characters where possible. This familiarises you with the salient characters of the animals (including measurements) and can be useful when using non-expert help.
- learn the local names for the species you expect, and for colours and body parts. Learn local names for pieces of equipment you will be using.
- familiarise yourself with your equipment - especially how it might be repaired "on the run".
- if you have not trapped small mammals before, try out your field techniques and analysis (where appropriate) before you leave.
- design and test field data sheets that allow you to collect information in a way that can be analysed easily (and are appropriate where possible for statistical tests).

- work out a labelling regime for your specimens in advance.

- though field experiments, and keeping animals in captivity, are generally inappropriate for most field expeditions, if planning such work follow the guidelines adopted by the Association for the Study of Animal Behaviour (Cuthill, 1991).

When undertaking literature research do not ignore older volumes of journals and old books as these often contain techniques highly appropriate to the conditions which expeditions work under.

For planning conservation fieldwork prioritisation of target species and the information needed about them can be found by referring to the appropriate IUCN/SSC action plan and the IUCN red list of threatened animals (Groombridge, 1993; Lidicker,1989; Nicoll & Rathbun, 1990).

Finally, do not forget to add the cost of excess baggage for traps and equipment to your budget. Remembering that on the return flight your luggage may weigh more.

Section Two

TECHNIQUES

2.1 Trapping

Though there are other ways of studying small mammals (see Section 7), trapping is the basic and most widespread. This section covers the trap and what to do with it and also what to do with any animals you catch.

2.1.1 Which type of trap?

Live or Dead: The first thing to be decided is whether you wish to trap with snap (or break-back) traps or with live traps. The pros and cons are as follows:

- snap traps generally catch more animals (but see Hasson & Hoffmeyer, 1973)
- snap traps are generally lighter, less bulky and have simpler working mechanisms
- additional snap traps can often be purchased locally to augment or replenish the expedition supply
- snap traps are generally cheaper than live traps

BUT
- snap traps kill things
- they are non-selective
- they limit the type of data that can be collected

Snap traps, then, are good for the "quick and dirty" survey, live traps have moral superiority and provide a more flexible data set.

One of the main problems with snap traps is that, though they catch more, it is very difficult to make them selective. The bulk of the catch is likely to be one or two very common species; the skins and skulls of which may well already be filling up several drawfulls in museums. Besides, if you have done the preparatory work well, your notes, field keys and photographs should allow you to identify a specimen with reasonable certainty. If the area of study supports, or potentially supports, rare species (see Groombridge, 1993 for guidance) it is difficult to justify the risk involved in the deployment of any snap traps (or any other type of killing trap).

A general guideline for collection policy is **never take a specimen unless you absolutely have to**. They often are not needed, and widespread collecting may be difficult to reconcile with the ethos of the expedition and/or that of the area in which you are working (especially if it is a conservation area, where it may sully relations with locals who have been asked not to kill animals in the reserve).

2.2 Choosing the trap - the right trap for the right habitat

The size and type of trap will determine the types of animals you catch (see as examples Keshava Bhat & Sujatha, 1987; Maly & Cranford, 1985; Morris, 1968; Neal & Cock, 1969; Ohgushi, 1986; Schwan, 1986; Slade et al., 1993; Thompson & Macauley, 1987; West, 1985; Wiener & Smith, 1972). This is not only dependent on size-related criteria, but also because different species often display a preference for a particular trap type (see Hansson & Hoffmeyer 1973; Rose et al., 1977; Willan, 1986a). Even factors such as mesh size may be influential (see O'Farrel et al., 1994). For both live and dead traps, an all-metal construction is generally recommended.

Snap traps with a wooden base have a tendency to warp in the rain or in extreme heat and be less easy to clean. Also, termites seem to love them and can demolish the base in a few days. Varnishing wooden parts may help but you can only use the trap once fully dry and be sure the varnish will not melt (or become tacky) in the heat of your intended study site (check with manufacturers first). If you insist on using snap traps, Selfset are the best (see Section 13.2.1). Coming in two sizes, their all-metal construction is robust and the trigger mechanism is both sensitive, reliable and easy to set. This contrasts with the most widely available wooden based traps (Nipper and Little Nipper) which have distressing tendencies to fall apart and crush your fingers!

The Longworth is the most commonly used small mammal live trap in the UK. The design has been around a long time (Chitty & Kempson, 1949) and a wealth of hints and tips now exist. "Longworth technology" is discussed in detail by Gurnell & Flowerdew (1990). Longworths come in two parts (box and tunnel), which fit inside each other for ease of transport. Each trap 14cm x 6.5cm x 8.5cm when broken down (the tunnel fits inside the nest box). Like this you can carry 30 to 40 in a large rucksack. Quite robust, the small diameter of its tunnel (5.0 x 6.2cm) limits the catch to animals less than 700g. The box serves as a refuge for the captured animal. Numerous spares are available from the manufacturers (see Section 13.2.1) making them easy to repair.

A more recent all-plastic trap ('The Living Trip-Trap') looks very like a Longworth (having a nest box and tunnel), though the treadle mechanism is different. It is cheaper than the Longworth (£7.80 vs. £24.00 in November 1994), and lighter (200g vs. 250g) and a smaller version of this trap is available. The design is less robust than the Longworth, being more prone to fractures and cracks and easier for small mammals to chew their way out of. In addition, if wet, water tension between door and tunnel roof can hold the door in the open position. The plus behind the new design idea (that the captured animal could be seen inside without the trap being opened) is also rapidly lost as the plastic is rapidly scrabbled to opacity by the claws of captured small mammals. A new development from Rentokil is the 'Trap-Ease Mouse Trap' which is simple, robust, waterproof and cheap (£2.29, October 1994), but is unlikely to work on anything except the smoothest of surfaces and there is no room for nest material.

Shermans are simple box-shaped traps of metal sheet. They come in many sizes and varieties (both collapsible and rigid), two of the commonest being 50 x 62 x 165mm and 76 x 89 x 229mm. They also produce extended version for catching small mammals with extra long tails. Sherman's are easily transportable and weigh from 250g. The whole trap serves as a refuge but there is a simple treadle mechanism which bedding and bait can interfere with the action of (Churchfield, 1990). Ease of maintenance (spares can be purchased prior to the expedition), and the ability to fold up, make them the preferred trap for tropical expedition use. Though the collapsible varieties (folding down to a thickness of 15mm) have a tendency to collapse in the field after setting.

Havaharts are box-shaped traps of strong wire mesh available in a variety of sizes (the smallest of which "o", is the most suitable for small mammals). Very robust and with a simple treadle mechanism, the disadvantage is that their open construction offers the captured animal no protection from the weather, a potential source of increased mortality. The treadle mechanism is exceptionally sensitive, this makes it vulnerable to being set-off by heavy rainfall. Also live bait (as used for insectivores, Churchfield, 1990) can escape through the mesh.

2.3 Setting traps in the field

2.3.1 The preliminary survey

This should proceed any trapping. It allows for unencumbered exploration of potential study sites and for comparisons to be made with other vegetation types. It will also allow you to plan the logistics of your operation. If the other members of your team are going to be conducting fieldwork in similar habitats, this is the time to organise a rota of work so that your studies do not interfere with each other. Common sense dictates that the least damaging work gets carried out first.

2.3.2 Where to place the trap

Small mammals do not use areas randomly, well placed traps will enhance your chances of success (see Gurnell & Langbein, 1983; Norton, 1987; Rana, 1986). Avoid placing traps in open or exposed areas, small mammals prefer to run along the edge of things (the "edge effect"), and will generally run round the edge of a clearing rather than across it. They are also creatures of habit, so look for tunnels at the base of vegetation (in thick grass this may mean right down at root level), or paths across leaf litter, moss or soil. The edges of boulders and logs are also well worth checking. Apart from disturbed soil and vegetation you may also see slight oily marks left by the repeated passing of hairy bodies against rocks roots and stems, or perhaps small tufts of fur caught on plant spines.

Holes are generally in out-of-the-way places, at the bases of boulders or logs, under dense vegetation, or at the base of tree roots. If you find one, check that there isn't another exit/entrance nearby - trap both (just to frustrate you, some species block their holes when in residence). Look down the hole - if its got an accumulation of detritus in it, or is covered with a spiders web it is likely to be disused (small mammals have not yet heard the legend of Robert the Bruce). It may be useful to determine active burrows and runways using sand trays or powdered-slides (Boonstra *et al.,* 1992). This is especially useful if populations are at low densities, but probably inappropriate in grids.

Other signs of small mammal activity include chewed food or faecal deposits. Accumulations of obviously favoured food are well worth trapping (and, if of appropriate consistency, may be worth incorporating into the bait).

2.3.3 Positioning the trap

Small mammals generally scuttle. Strange objects may be investigated, but they hate to step *up* onto something. So keep the trap's leading edge flush with the ground; excavate a bit if you have to, angle the bulk of the trap appropriately, or prop it up with sticks or stones.

When trapping a steep bank you can balance the trap on a couple of sticks rammed firmly into the substrate. If you are trapping with box-like live traps on slopes angle it so that the bedding will be kept dry if it rains and water runs down the slope - otherwise your catch is liable to die of hypothermia.

If you are trapping holes or runs and positioning the trap "head-on" would create too much disturbance, try angling a couple of sticks from the site to the trap. The moving animal will often be deflected these stick-guides and run into (or onto) the trap. The Star-Trap technique (described in Section 2.3.8.4) is an extension of this simple, but effective idea.

When using snap trap make sure there is sufficient clearance for the bar to come over freely - otherwise the animal will escape when the bar gets snagged or slowed on overhanging vegetation. A bit of "gardening" may be called for - but don't disturb the area too much or the animals may avoid the place.

2.3.4 Spacing the traps

There are two main ways of arranging traps, by grid and by line. Trap lines are useful when covering a large number of habitats at one time, trying to detect movement between adjacent habitats or in linear habitats (e.g. hedgerows)(see Southern, 1965). Apart from providing an index it is difficult to calculate population densities and traps will probably require closer spacing (Gurnell & Flowerdew, 1990). Trap grids are a pre-requisite for population size, density and home range studies. Square grids are standard with traps being equi-distance from each other. Grid trapping introduces the 'edge-effect' when more captures in traps around the edge occur (Flowerdew, 1976; Gurnell & Flowerdew, 1990). To overcome this the outer trap captures could be ignored, though this can mean larger grids and correspondingly greater trap numbers. With both trap patterns it is possible to take the rigid or the flexible approach. With the first the trapping is done from the exact point given by the predetermined spacing, in the second this point is used as a guideline and traps placed in suitable spots nearby. Gurnell & Flowerdew (1990) suggest spacing to be 5m in grassland, 10m or 15m in woodland and 20m in arable habitats. Tew *et al.,* (1994b) discuss the effects of trap spacing and suggest wider spacings and longer trapping periods for projects with a limited number of traps.

It is normal to position more than one trap at each point (trapping station). A variety of sizes and types increases the chance of success. Only using one size of trap increases the chance of missing part of the small mammal fauna. If working with live traps it is common to place them back to back in a run (as most snap traps can be approached from any angle this does not apply).

2.3.5 How many traps?

This is difficult to assess until you have an idea of your trapping success rates. Gurnell & Flowerdew (1990) consider that, as a rule of thumb, if 50%-60% of your traps are filled at one time then more traps should be put down.

If using the minimum number alive estimate of population (Gurnell & Flowerdew, 1990) this assumes that a high proportion of the population has been trapped. This requires high sampling effort with a high density of traps over a large area, with 50% remaining empty on any one occasion.

Even with low trap rates (0.5 to 1%), two to three hundred traps is about all you'll be able to do in a day, as traps will have to be checked, rebaited, replaced or searched for. The catch will have to be processed too.

The location of the trap site will also regulate the number of traps available. Remote sites with no means of trap carrying other than rucsacs mean fewer, while easily accessible sites or the use of pack animals/vehicle transport mean more can be carried. The mammal team on the UEA São Tomé expedition found that 40 Longworths along with bait etc. and camping gear for 10 days was impossible for two people to carry. It is a matter of logistics and the expedition should be planned accordingly.

2.3.6 Tying, marking and tagging
You should be able to find your traps quickly and easily; this is especially important when losing time delays the release of animals from live traps. Disturbance to vegetation, associated with a fruitless search, can also prejudice subsequent trap success.

Firstly, it is important that the trap is securely tied to an immovable object to avoid its removal by a carnivore or it being dragged by a "zombie" (an animal caught in a snap trap, but not killed outright). Use either a stake or a nearby bush. Attach using a slip knot. Use nylon string rather than natural fibres as it has greater tensile strength and does not perish or get eaten by ants or termites. To avoid snagging the line on a moving trap part, drill a hole in the trap body. Alternatively peg the traps down with tent pegs or croquet hoop shaped metal rod. In extreme cases of disturbance an enclosure similar to that described by Layne (1987) could be used, however this increases the weight and bulk of equipment to be carried.

If you are working in open habitats (e.g. grasslands) a simple tag is sufficient, sequentially numbered and fixed at a height so as to be visible from both proceeding and subsequent trap stations. Ideally tags should be brightly coloured, waterproof and numbered in indelible pen. The orange tape used to mark road constructions is ideal - see Sections 13.1.7 and 13.2.7.

Closed habitats (e.g. rainforest) often have a visual horizon that is less than the inter-trap distance. Here "festooning" is a good option; a length of thin cord is run at chest height for the whole length of the trap line (or part of grid). The trap ties are run off from this mainline (using a running loop to avoid accidents) and tied to the traps via pre-drilled holes (done prior to the expedition). Tags are tied at the junction of the trap tie and mainline. Though this method adds to the time taken to the setting-up and taking-down times, it saves a great deal of operating time. Nylon is the best material for the cord being both rot-proof and unattractive to termites. Be sure to take away the cord when you have finished.

Some workers number the actual traps using painted numbers or a colour code. However, unless the same order is adhered to, this can lead to confusion when traps are used again later. If marking the traps is essential stick on a piece of insulating tap (which is easily removed) and mark this.

2.3.7 How long to trap an area?
This depends entirely on what you wish to do and how many traps you have. However, "optimum giving up times" can be calculated by plotting return-for-effort; for live traps this is the number of new individuals trapped vs. number of retraps, for snap traps the tailing off in the number of animals caught. You do not always get your biggest catch on the first night - the strange objects may be avoided by the animals for a while (see Section 2.4.4). Two hundred trap nights (no. traps x no. nights) is a good minimum.

Even if you are at a site for a short while try not to overlook the smaller habitat types (e.g. Weisel & Brandl, 1993). They may represent only a small part of the area you are working in, but they may have unique species. For example, some species (e.g. *Phyllotis*, in the Andes and *Trichomys* in the Brazilian cerrado) favour rock outcrops and seldom move far from them. Other species (e.g. *Dactylomys*) favour bamboo groves, still others prefer (e.g. *Sigmodon*) marshes or wet grasslands (e.g. *Calomys*). Your pre-fieldwork literature search should have alerted you to such possibilities.

You may find it more rewarding to trap one or two localities for a longer time rather than flitting between several (and losing work time in travelling as a consequence). In general, the longer you trap one locality the more representative your sample(s) will be. Even long-term studies show this relationship; for example, Alho *et al.,* (1986) trapped in Brazilian cerrado (grass/scrub mix) for four years and recorded 25 species of small mammal, while Deitz (1983) trapped the same habitat type for 17 months and recorded only 10 species. Remember, moonlight can greatly reduce trapping success (see Lockard & Owins, 1974a,b) so do not be surprised by periodic lows in trap success.

2.3.8 Special trapping techniques

2.3.8.1 Arboreal traps

Arboreal trapping is an important component of a faunal inventory, especially in tropical forests. For example Mabberly (1983) has estimated that some 85% of the mammal fauna of Borneo is arboreal. An inventory that does not deal with this component is very far from complete (see also McClearn *et al.,* 1994 and references therein).

Despite guides to tree climbing (e.g. Mitchell, 1982), access can be a major problem. Time spent ascending and descending trees greatly limits the number of trees that can be set and checked on a daily basis. It is very difficult to set as many traps as one would in a ground-based survey. One way round this is to use the pulley-and-platform system devised by Jay Malcolm (see Malcolm, 1991). He also describes an additional modification to the traps which should allow you to rig-up a small flag-like indicator that will tell you when the trap is sprung (on the same principle as American mail boxes).

A programme using Malcolm's Technique obviously requires major effort and investment in time, materials and planning. It is not something that is approached half-heartedly. A less demanding option is to get into the canopy direct but use the slopes of a hill to do so directly, or lower yourself over the lip of a cliff onto canopy below. Traps can then be checked directly. Topography may mitigate against this.

Arboreal trapping involving tree climbing may not be advisable for expeditions to remote areas. The potential for serious accidents is greatly increased, no matter how careful or experienced the team members are. If tree climbing is to be part of the expedition's activities it is advisable to go on a tree climbing course such as those run by Merrist Wood Agricultural College (see Section 13.2.9).

If not using the pulley-and-platform system traps may be positioned directly in trees and affixed directly to the trunk. Traps may be lashed with cord or pinned in place by nails on either side of the trap body. With snap traps make sure these do not interfere with the working mechanism of the trap. Since arboreal animals have an extra dimension in which to avoid the trap and are generally much more agile than terrestrial ones, positioning of the trap is crucial. If it is not done right an animal may simply leap over it (McClearn *et al.,* 1994 found that half of their arboreal traps never caught anything). Runs can be best detected in moss where they show up as beaten down pathways (see Carey & Witt, 1991). On branches with larger amounts of epiphytic vegetation check for grease marks on leaves and bits of fur caught on spines. Put the treadle end of the trap flush with the substrate (you may have to make a sort of cat's-cradle arrangement to do this). Traps can also be tied onto the main trunk (remember that most small mammals descend the trunk head down). If the trunk has a very large girth try attaching it via strings tied to pegs or nails driven into the trunk (note when you have finished make sure to put a drop of fungicide and sealant into the holes). Do not forget to take all the standard anti-ant precautions (26 genera and 43 species of ant have been found living in a single tree in the Peruvian Amazon [Wilson, 1987], equivalent to the entire ant fauna of all habitats in the British Isles! - see Section 2.5.1 for anti-ant techniques). There are plenty of arboreal carnivores - so make sure the traps cannot be dragged away (see Section 2.5.2).

Mammal distributions in the forest are vertically stratified (Charles-Dominique *et al.,* 1981; Malcolm, 1991; McClearn *et al.,* 1994), so keep an accurate record of trap height.

If you are pushed then choose only those trees in fruit at the time of your visit (checking the ground for fallen fruit will help here as will talking to local people). Palms are often especially worthy of attention in this context.

It is probably inadvisable to use a gun to bring down specimens from the trees. Though formerly a widely used collecting method it is very rarely employed today. Unless you are a particularly good shot you are unlikely to succeed (especially in thick forest). In many countries the possession of guns is likely to be misinterpreted by local authorities. It may also be difficult to rationalise its use with the conservation ethos that (one would hope) the expedition would seek to convey to local communities.

2.3.8.2 Aerial traps

When carrying out a trapping programme many researchers only position traps on the ground, neglecting potential niches in long grass, bushes etc. Investigating such areas does not have the logistical and safety implications attached to arboreal trapping. By fixing traps approximately 1m above ground in reedbeds a UEA project increased its capture success of harvest mice (*Micromys minutus*).

Tattersall & Whitbread (1994) found that 20% of woodmice (*Apodemus sylvaticus*) and 14% of bank voles (*Muscardinus avellanarius*) were captured off the ground. They also found that 17% of captures of juvenile bank voles occurred off ground. Morris & Whitbread (1986) found that capture success of the dormouse (*Muscardinus avellanarius*) increased by using traps placed at heights between 1 and 3.5m. The live capture of the bamboo rat

(*Kannabateomys amblyonyx*) was only possible by placing traps off ground on bamboo bridges (Kierulff *et al.,* 1991).

It is possible that the methodology may bias the results. Some species are known to enter the first trap they encounter, thus ground placed traps may reduce the recorded incidence of arboreality (Montgomery, 1980a). However, by not using aerial trap placement you may miss segments of the small mammal population, biasing any species lists and invalidating population size estimates.

In bushes and scrub, traps could be directly attached to branches, in long grass strap to bamboo canes or similar. It may be easier to use one-piece traps (e.g. Sherman's). Take care not to cause undue disturbance or damage and remember to record the height at which traps are placed (and the height of the vegetation being trapped).

2.3.8.3 Aquatic traps

Aquatic small mammals form a small, but very interesting part of the fauna. They are often very little known and therefore worthy of study.

The three best places to trap are runs in riverside vegetation, holes in the riverbank and climb-out sites. The latter are normally situated where the bank or beach slopes more callously, alternatively rocks in the middle of watercourses may be tried. Piles of faeces, mud worn smooth, and tracks in the gravel or sand should all be searched for.

If live trapping ensure that there is one part of the trap that will remain dry should the trap move from its position or the river level rise. One modification is to add a length of stiff pipe to the back of the trap (firmly sealing off the far end first). Such pipes, pushed through a hole cut in the back of the trap, fitted with a rubber sleeve at the join, and secured with a pair of small L-shaped metal brackets (attached with bolts with the head facing in), can help in such incidents by providing a dry retreat. Stoddart (1970) gives a design for a water vole *Arvicola terrestris* live trap.

All traps beside running water should be securely fastened on the bank and the trap tie string given a couple of turns around the body of the trap for extra security (fitting customised lugs is an alternative). For extra security buttress the trap with stones to prevent its movement or peg down as mentioned in Section 2.3.6).

Traps on floating platforms are an alternative. A trap is securely fastened to a large wooden platform which is then attached by a cord to the stream bed. The platform should be large enough to be stable with the weight of an animal on it or in the trap. Take account of the possibility of storms and consequent rapid rises in water level when deciding on the length of cord (see also Baker & Clarke, 1988). Stirton (1944) constructed small weirs with which to catch fishing mice.

Several investigators having had no luck with conventional traps have found that local wicker fish traps can be effective. It is worth talking to local people knowledgeable in fishing techniques for information, possibilities and ideas.

2.3.8.4 Star trap

This is a modification to the standard snap trapping technique and uses the stick-guide idea mentioned previously (see Section 2.3.3). It is appropriate for forest-floor use and is especially useful for areas of very low small mammal density (see da Cunha & Barnett, 1988).

A shallow pit is excavated in the substrate of sufficient size and depth that the surface of the trap is flush with the substrate surface. Sticks, twigs and other impeding detritus of note is then removed in a radius of 1m around the trap. Six to eight natural poles slightly longer than this are then gathered and arranged radially around the trap, one end touching the trap, the other lying outside the cleaned area of ground. The ends of the poles should not touch each other.

This arrangement exploits the predilection of small mammals for moving with their bodies in contact with a horizontal object (the edge effect). In guiding the animals into the trap area the poles increase the effective catchment area of the trap and thus increase trap success. A modification is to dig a bigger pit and use four traps. This increases the directional response of the system. It should also be adaptable for use with live traps.

This style of trapping is not novel; those tiny carnivorous plants, the bladderworts (Ultriculariaceae), got there first.

2.3.8.5 Smoking-out

This is useful for hollow trees, logs or rock jumbles which would be difficult to access with standard traps. The results are not easily quantified but it may yield species you would otherwise miss and so are useful if inventories are being constructed.

Check the area first, mark all possible holes and securely fix nets over them (mist nets are appropriate, fishing nets are generally too coarse or of materials which can cut and injure a struggling animal). Light a small fire at the base of the primary hole and then cover it with green leaves. The resulting thick smoke should drive out sheltering animals.

Once in the net animals can be disentangles and then processed as any other live-trapped capture. Anaesthetics should be administered with care as the animal may already be stressed by the smoke.

Two words of caution - you may get quite large animals this way, thick gloves are a wise precaution. Also, be very careful you do not start a more widespread conflagration than you anticipated

2.3.8.6 Netting

The technique, where nets are set up in a half-circle and animals driven into them by a group beating the vegetation is no longer widely used. It is non-selective, disruptive and traumatising. Also it tends to be more successful in catching larger mammals.

However the use of nets is still practised to capture some elephant shrew species (Fitzgibbon & Rathbun, 1994; Hanna & Anderson, 1993; Rathbun, 1979). 25m-45m long, 2m high 7cm mesh nets are strung along paths with over half of the net laid on the ground. The animals run into the net and become entangled. Nets are checked every 2-4 hours and captured animals removed (see Hanna & Anderson, 1993).

2.3.9 Special considerations for live traps

Before setting the trap always check the inside for any inwards-facing damage (e.g. proud rivets or seams) that could harm the captive animal. Rodents can chew through the metal of box traps like Longworths. If you can't patch them (an old piece of tin can and araldite is good in an emergency), then at least file off the rough edges as they can be harmful to occupants. A range of spares are available for both Longworth and Sherman traps and it may be wise to take an assortment (see Section 13.2.1).

If the object of your live trapping is to re-release your captures, you should provide bedding and food sufficient for their period of incarceration. Bedding can be anything non-toxic and warming, old newspaper, dried leaves or hay have all been used. Do not put in plant material with spines or which might be toxic or have caustic latex. Non-absorbent cotton wool is especially useful in wet environments, and has the added advantage of reducing mortality in shrews (Churchfield, 1990; Gurnell & Flowerdew, 1990). Do not put in anything that is wet or damp - this will chill the animal and could kill it (this is true even in the tropics). The UEA São Tomé expedition had difficulty keeping bedding dry, despite collecting and storing in plastic bags. It may be worth taking silica gel to absorb condensation. When placing bedding in traps without separate nest boxes (e.g. Shermans) be careful not to foul the action of the treadle.

Food can be extra bait placed in with the bedding, this avoids death by starvation which can be a particular problem for insectivorous mammals. It is not generally necessary to provide water. Rag soaked with water has been provided by some workers, however.

A metal box is not as warm as a burrow and specimen death through hypothermia can be a real problem in cold climates. Extra insulation can be provided by attaching (permanently or temporarily) polystyrene sheets around the box to form an insulating jacket (see also Shaw & Milner, 1967). Alternatively, the sheeting can be applied just to the underside of the trap for ground insulation (such philanthropy also has the useful result of making the traps less painful to handle).

If using live traps of the open cage design, try to place one part beneath something or attach cardboard or plastic sheeting to offer some protection in case of inclement weather or strong sun. Even with solid traps it is worth placing them out of direct sunlight in hot climates.

In hot open habitats painting the trap with a pale coloured paint may help to alleviate heat stress for any captured occupant.

Be aware that some species may have their tail damaged when the door is sprung. If you are likely to capture animals with extra long tails it would make sense to take steps to remedy this. Sherman produce an extra long trap just for this purpose.

2.4 Bait

2.4.1 Which bait?

The type of bait can greatly effect the type and numbers of the catch (see, for example, Willan, 1986b). Bait is a matter of experimentation, but a widely used (and successful) bait consists of porridge oats, peanut butter, water and cooking oil mixed to the consistency of stiff cake mix. Locally available fruit can be added to provide a wider spectrum. To attract carnivorous (or insectivorous) species tinned meats, fresh meat (from specimens), or tinned fish (not in tomato sauce) can be added or used on its own. However Churchfield (1990) states that tinned or dried dog food is not eaten regularly, if at all, by shrews. It may therefore be an idea to collect local invertebrates for inclusion into the bait. Contrary to popular opinion rodents do not appear inordinately fond of cheese.

Where the majority of the species are confirmed grain eaters (e.g. deserts), sunflower seeds, corn or wheat have been used successfully in their simple dry state.

Piscivorous species can be caught on fresh local fish or tinned fish, though animals have been caught on the standard mix described above.

At a distance rodents detect food by its smell (Pennycuik & Cowan, 1990), so it is best not prepare bait if you have just handled anything very pungent, perfumed, spicy or mechanically oily. Small mammals do not generally like such odours.

2.4.2 How much bait?

For a snap trap a piece the size of a golf ball should do fifteen to twenty traps. Putting a lot of bait on the trigger means that you have to compensate for the weight by setting the tripping mechanism less sensitively. Large volumes of bait increases the chances of attracting non-target species like birds, snails and insects.

When baiting a live trap remember that rodents have a rapid metabolism and you are providing both attractant and feed. The attractant can be as above, the feed should be about 10% of the weight of the biggest thing you expect to catch in the trap.

2.4.3 How often to bait?

Change or replenish the bait every day if it is a moist mix, when required if it is a dry one. If bait gets blood on it change it.

NOTE: if a snap trap has lost its bait, do not attempt to rebait the trap while it is set. Set it off with a stick, rebait and reset.

2.4.4 Baiting before trapping

Many small mammals are cautious of new things (see Barnett, 1981 and Cowan & Barnett, 1975 for reviews; Bammer et al., 1988 and Chopra & Sood, 1984 as examples), though some are not (e.g. Churchfield, 1990 and Gurnell & Flowerdew 1990 for shrews; Cowan, 1977 for rodents). To avoid bias in results, many authors like to bait before trapping to give the more cautious species the time and opportunity to grow more confident.

2.4.4.1 Pre-baiting

The already positioned traps are baited for one to several days before the traps are set. The idea is that animals will be attracted by the free meal, begin to visit the traps on a regular basis and so more will be caught when trapping begins.

The technique has its proponents and detractors (see Alibhai & Key, 1985; Gurnell, 1977, 1980 and references therein). It is worth remembering that it will probably attract animals from neighbouring areas, giving a false impression of density and, perhaps, of relative species composition. Live-trap studies of density and home-range size are likely to be prejudiced under such conditions. It is best regarded a way of increasing trap success - but not necessarily the representativeness of the data. The problem of attracting neighbouring animals may be negated by discounting captures from the outer traps (see Section 2.3.4).

2.4.4.2 Groundbaiting

This is an extreme form of pre-baiting, where small bits of bait are strewn over the general area to be worked in advance of the initiation of trapping. While this probably results in even greater distortion of the data away from "the real situation", it is useful in situations where small mammal density is exceptionally low and return for trapping effort would otherwise be prohibitively low (Barnett & da Cunha, 1994).

NOTE: Malhi & Parshad (1994) have used, with success, a technique of below ground pre-baiting for areas of high incidences of non-target species.

2.5 Unexpected hazards

2.5.1 Problems with unwanted guests

You are very likely to catch non-target species. Ground-foraging birds, large snails, reptiles and amphibians, all may get caught by accident or because they were attracted to the bait (see da Cunha & Barnett, 1988; McClearn *et al.*, 1994; Read, 1987). There is little that you can do about this (except keep good records as, obviously, it effects your calculations of trap success - see Section 12.2). Covering snap traps with a 'roof' or placing them in boxes may help to prevent the capture or injury of non-target species.

However, some visitors are much less welcome; especially in rainforests a persistent problem may be encountered with ants who visit the trap and remove the bait (McClearn *et al.*, 1994). On occasion this can be a major factor in reducing trap success (da Cunha & Barnett, 1988; Barnett & da Cunha, 1994). In extreme cases they may hurt or kill a captive animal (see Masser & Grant, 1986). There are two ways to deal with it: use cotton wool soaked in macerated fruit (which gives an attractive smell, but nothing the ants can steal), or use normal bait with a repellent (e.g. Anderson & Ohmart, 1977; Chabreck *et al.*, 1986). Beltyukova & Spassky (1989) give a design for an ant-proof trap.

Cotton wool techniques should not be used for live traps as any trapped animal will then have nothing to eat.

2.5.2 Other problems - visitors

Soldier ants - these migratory ants come in hoards that are carnivorous, unstoppable and totally destructive. If any come through an area you are trapping, get out and change your project to one of "post-infestation recolonization by small mammals".

Termites - termites attack wooden traps. Insecticides also appear to repel small mammals, use metal traps or rapidly rotate traps between stockpile and field to avoid their demolition.

Carnivore theft - a canny carnivore may well begin to use your traps as a restaurant (see Lightfoot & Wallis, 1982). If you have not pegged down your traps sufficiently well then you may lose these as well (see Section 2.3.6). Repellents (pepper, urine, carnivore faeces) are likely to discourage the small mammals as well. Either move the traps or put out a special, large, plate of food for the carnivore to satiate it.

Human theft - is very difficult to deal with in well-populated areas (where one solution is to mark the locations on a map, and not at all in the field). In rural areas, a change in tagging procedure may work - but talking to local people is even better.

Layne (1987) describes an enclosure for protecting small mammal traps against disturbance by the likes of cattle, pigs etc. On an expedition this is likely to be a heavy investment in time and resources. In such extreme situations it is probably better simply to pack up and move elsewhere.

2.5.3 Other problems - weather

Day to day variation in the weather influences small mammal activity and hence their trappability. Small mammal activity is less on bright moonlight nights (Lockard & Owings, 1974a), cold nights (Getz, 1968; Vickery & Bider, 1978), or nights with heavy rain (Mystkowska & Sidorowicz, 1961). Small insectivores may be more active on warm moist nights (Doucet & Bider, 1974; Pankakoski, 1979), and increased activity following rain has been reported for shrews (Doucet & Bider, 1974), rodents (Vickery & Bider, 1981) and small marsupials (Goldingay & Denny, 1986). Wind can also effect trapping success (Bowland, 1987). Resulting differences in trappability can be of an order of magnitude. It is consequently worth noting the weather in your field note book. It also a reason for not panicking if you get unexpectedly low trap success at some stage while trapping a site. Weather and moonphase also influence detectability when spotlighting animals (Goldingay & Kavanagh, 1988; Laurance, 1990).

Seasonal variation also effects small mammal activity (see Stephenson, 1994). Low trappability at certain times of the year can be commonly be attributed to:

- the fact that (in hot dry climates) the animals are aestivating
- cyclic nature of the populations (decrease in actual density)
- an increased home range (decrease in apparent density)
- a change in feeding habits

Flemming (1971, 1973) has shown that trappability may be increased in the dry season, while Barnett & da Cunha (1994), da Cunha & Barnett (1988), and Read (1988) found that low densities of dry-season small mammal communities resulted in very low trap success (see also McClearn, 1994). Heavy fruit falls may also have a strong influence on absolute numbers and trappability of animals (see Barnett & da Cunha, 1994 and references therein). Low soil fertility may be an ultimate causal factor for reduced numbers of small mammals in some areas (Emmons, 1984). Responses to moonlight (see above) may show seasonality (see Lockard & Owings, 1974b, c), as may levels of diurnal activity (Renolds & Gorman, 1994).

Some of the variations to which the animals are responding may be supra-annual and only detectable by a long term study (see Pucek *et al.*, 1993 as a fine example).

2.5.4 Other problems - trapping bias

There are many sources of bias, even in traps which are well-positioned and correctly set. Some of these are dealt with elsewhere (trap-type 2.2, bait type 2.4.1, bait removal 2.5.1, odour 2.8.9).

Bias effects both the species composition of the catch and the age and sex composition of the trapped individuals (see Davies & Emlen, 1956; Summerlin & Wolff, 1973). If you wish to draw any conclusions about the social behaviour of the regions small mammals, you should be aware that:

- young, dispersing sub-adults are more likely to enter traps than other age-classes (Summerlin & Wolff, 1973)
- adult males are more likely to enter traps than adult females (e.g. Hansson, 1975)
- pregnant and lactating females move about little.
- weight associated biases occur (e.g. Boonstra & Rodd, 1982; Witt, 1991)

These factors influence trap results by altering the likelihood of trap encounter, but there are other factors too. These include: reduced trappability in some chromosomal varieties (e.g. Gérard, *et al.*, 1994), higher trappability of large bodied socially dominant males (e.g. Wolff, 1993) and the effects of interspecific territoriality (Feldhammer *et al.*, 1993; Wolff *et al.*, 1983).

For grids there are also a number of effects relating to the traps position in the grid (O'Farrell *et al.*, 1977).

2.6 Other types of trap

2.6.1 Pit fall traps

Pit fall traps are simply plastic or metal containers (on the lines of buckets, commercial coffee tins or traffic cones) sunk into the ground (see Bennett *et al.*, 1989). They should be deep enough so that animals cannot leap out of them, about 30cm deep for shrews and voles, deeper for more agile species (adding a an inwards-pointing lip around the edge of the trap helps here). Their use is obviously limited to places with a sufficiently deep substrate in which they can be buried (difficult in stony deserts, for example). They are not selective and can catch more than one animal (Boonstra & Krebs, 1978). The disadvantage of this is that comparability with other trapping systems is difficult and statistical analysis is complicated by the fact that most packages have been developed for 'single shot' traps (see Section 12.2). However they do often get animals that 'standard' traps do not (a team of mammalogists in Cameroon, greatly frustrated by their inability to catch elephant shrews in their traps, met with rather mixed emotions the news from the expeditions herpetologist that he averaged several elephant shrews a day in his pit-falls - see also Mengak & Guynn, 1987; Singleton, 1987 for examples and Williams & Braun, 1983 for review).

NOTE that some species e.g. shrews and *Peromyscus* avoid pit fall traps after the initial capture (Twigg, 1975a).

As with any other kind of live trap baiting is preferred - to provide food for the prisoner(s). As the traps are non selective, material should be placed in the bottom to provide hiding places for the smaller captures (when checking the trap always look for evidence of other animals that may have been eaten by the survivors). Remove any sticks that fall in as the captives may climb up them and escape. Pitfalls can capture animals other than small mammals; it is unwise to simply to plunge your naked hand into the bucket - there may be a cross, poisonous, snake at the bottom.

These traps are very prone to flooding, captives are liable to die by drowning or from hypothermia. Try to avoid slopes or obvious water channels where possible. Positioning, upslope, of sticks or other materials to divert rain flows can help. If rain is expected a roof, a few centimetres larger in diameter than the trap, should cover the hole. This should be supported 3-5cm off the ground e.g. by stones and weighed down so it does not blow off. Such covers would also be useful to keep sunlight off.

For increased effectiveness the star trap technique could be adapted, with sticks radiating from the trap (see Section 2.3.8.4).

2.6.2 Drift nets

To enhance the performance of traps a continuous piece of non-perishable material is run through the trapping site. Supported on stakes (attached at brass bound eyelet's if possible, see Sections 13.1.11 and 13.2.9) at regular intervals, and dug into the ground (to provide additional support and prevent anything from crawling underneath), this technique exploits the 'edge effect' (see Section 2.3.2) by providing an artificial one. Traps (live, snap or pitfall) are positioned at regular intervals along the length of the drift net. They may be positioned on both sides in a staggered formation. Examples of drift net use include Banta (1957), Braithwaite (1983), Cockburn et al., (1978), Friend (1984) and Luff (1975).

Though this technique is useful for increasing trapping success in areas of low small mammal density (and, as such is very useful to expeditions working in remote, little known areas), its use inputs a bias and falls foul of many of the assumptions upon which many of the techniques of statistical analysis are based. This may not matter too much for expeditions whose main aim is to make an inventory, but should be taken into account if population studies are being undertaken.

Care should be exercised when positioning the drift net. If boundaries between vegetation types are crossed then estimations of habitat specificity by small mammal species may be excessively blurred as a result.

2.6.3 Bottle traps

The design for this simple and cheap live trap is outlined below. It can be easily made with local materials and used to supplement any traps you bring with you. The major advantage is that it has no mechanical parts, a disadvantage is that, if badly made, it can be dangerous to the captured animals.

2.6.3.1 Making a bottle trap

This is real Blue Peter stuff. Take a plastic bottle (a washing up bottle or similar will do). Slice it through about one-third of the way up. One part should then fit over the other like a sleeve. Cut a hole about 4 cm diameter low down about 1.5 cm from the base.

Take a piece of stiff plastic tube about 4cm in diameter and about 10cm long. Make two holes opposite each other in the midline of the tube. To these attach, via a small bolt, some thin springy metal sheet. It should have the following shape:

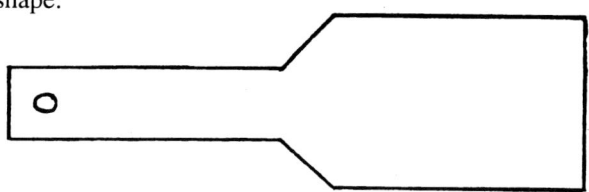

The distal ends of the bits of metal sheet should touch. The bolts should be head inwards with the neck pointing outwards. The nut is tightened on the outside of the tube. Make two more holes in the sides of the bottle and push the ends of the bolts through. Fix them (and the tube) with another nut. This should hold the tube in place. If it does not (perhaps because of the curve of the bottle or because the plastic is thin), try fitting a rubber ring around the tube to act as a sealing sleeve (glue is not a nice idea as it can hurt a captive animal).

The entire operating mechanism of this trap depends on the springiness of the metal you use for the doors. Effectively, you are making a very simple one-way valve which the animal will force open but which (if the metal is thick enough) it should not be able to reopen once on the other side. If the tube is 4cm diameter then the doors should be 4cm high. Make sure that you smooth off all rough edges, otherwise any captured animal could cut itself. To get your animal out, simply separate the two bits of the former washing-up bottle (you might wish to make some matching holes and insert a bit of stick through all four for extra security).

This trap may sound primitive and a bit Heath Robinson-ish. But it does work and provides a very simple cheap live trap that is easily made from locally available materials. However, the bottles are generally only good for two to four captures before they get chewed up.

2.6.4 Variations on a theme
It would appear that few workers can resist the temptation to build a better mouse trap. Consequently a great number of new designs and modifications are published each year. Many are modifications for specific species (e.g. Duckworth *et al.,* 1987; Gates *et al.,* 1988; Hickman, 1979; Morris &

Whitbread, 1986; Timchenko, 1986), or types of animal (e.g. Kinnear *et al.,* 1988), or specific reasons (Beltyukova & Spassky, 1987; Gates & Tanner, 1988), or just new designs (e.g. le Boulenge & le Boulenge-Nguyen, 1987; Davis, 1961; Schipanov, 1987; Stoddart, 1970; Timchenko, 1987; Willan, 1979). Check the literature for such non-standard applications, there may be just the thing you need. This will also show accessories that may be of aid in your work (e.g. Bekker, 1986 on how to construct a time-clock for a Longworth trap; Blotekjaer *et al.,* 1978 on an automatic passage-registering device). For a general overview of trap designs see Bateman (1971).

2.7 Checking the trap

2.7.1 How often?
Never ever leave live traps unattended for more than 12 hours. If the check cannot be done, close up the traps.

Most species of small mammal are nocturnal or crepuscular (active at sunrise and sunset), so traps are normally checked at dawn and at dusk. It is not general practice to check during the night as this can disturb the animals (and, in remote places, be dangerous for the investigator). A mid-day check is generally unrewarding, but is worth it if a major part of the fauna is diurnal (your pre-expedition literature search should alert you to this possibility). Note, levels of diurnal activity may show seasonal fluctuations (e.g. Reynolds & Gorman, 1994).

Insectivores have a very high metabolic rate, and if they are likely to form a large proportion of your catch or they are the main focus of your work, traps **must** be checked more frequently (Gurnell & Flowerdew, 1990). Churchfield (1990) recommends four visits per day (dawn, midday, late afternoon and evening) and the provision of suitable food and bedding will allow survival for up to 10 hours overnight.

The shock of capture can be great for a small mammal (Guthrie *et al.,* 1967; Rosenberg & Anthony, 1993) also, because their high metabolic rates, they may die in a few hours if not released (see Montgomery, 1980b; Perrin, 1975). Stress related weight-loss, following prolonged confinement, may mean long-term survival can also be effected (Kaufman & Kaufman, 1994; Schon & Korn, 1992).

2.7.2 How?
Checking snap traps is not difficult. Success is generally immediately visible. Consider the possibility of "zombie" animals and carry an euthanasia kit (see below). Always record if traps were set off but did not catch anything (if it is

a big problem you may have to account for it in your analysis). Has the bait gone? Are there any other signs of activity (e.g. faeces, hair, paw marks - see Twigg, 1975a)? If yes, then replace the trap with a bigger or stronger one.

Unless the live trap is of the cage variety it is not always easy to tell if a sprung trap is a successful one. Before opening, it is best to listen for movement first, then pick it up (gently).

2.7.3 What to record immediately

The following data should be recorded in the field note book (and copied up later): habitat type, trap number, trap location, date, time, species, sex, ectoparasites. Additional notes may be made on trap type and bait type. If the trap has been set off but nothing caught then this too should be recorded, as should any non-target species that is caught (e.g. snails or lizards).

2.8 Specimen processing

2.8.1 Getting an animal out of a live trap

Animals do not generally like being trapped and are unlikely to be co-operative. Nothing is more frustrating than finding the trap full, opening it and then watching the fur flash by as your capture escapes. Nothing is more embarrassing than to get a close look at your specimen only because it has just clamped its jaws to your thumb. There is also the (slim) chance of more than one animal in the trap (one winter AB got 23 fieldmice in 20 Longworth traps - see also Bergstrom, 1986; Bergstrom & Sauer, 1986; Montgomery, 1979). To avoid traumatising the animal it may be best to lightly anaesthetise it before processing (see next section).

Twigg (1975a) illustrates a technique for removing an animal from a Longworth by hand. On an expedition this may not be wise as you never quite know if the trap contains a nice cuddly mammal or an angry poisonous beasty! This technique may also be difficult for those who are anatomically disadvantaged (broad palms, short fingers). The plastic bag technique is more advisable for extracting animals from traps (Gurnell & Flowerdew, 1990; Twigg, 1975a). This can either be done by placing the whole trap inside an sufficiently large plastic bag, opening the trap and gently shaking out the contents, or by placing the trap mouth in the bag opening and then shaking. If you are using traps with a tunnel and nest box be aware that on occasions animals can remain in the tunnel, therefore either check and gently 'blow' them into the nest box or use the former variation on the plastic bag technique. Whichever variation, be sure to grasp the bag opening tightly as the ease with which some captives escape puts even Houdini to shame. Once the animal is in the bag it is then possible to manoeuvre it into a corner and remove the trap and most of the bedding.

For slightly larger mammals and those which it is undesirable to come into contact with their urine or be bitten by (such as the Norway rat *Rattus norvegicus*) emptying the trap into a cloth bag and then using a handling cone may be advisable (Twigg, 1975a). See Section 2.8.3.

2.8.2 Anaesthesia

For some prolonged procedures, such as ear tagging (e.g. Salamon & Klettenheimer, 1994), it may be necessary to immobilise captured animals. It is also not unheard of for nervous species to expire while being handled. To avoid such trauma and to make animals easier to handle it may be advantageous to anaesthetise them. Anyone planning to use anaesthesia during their studies should check for any relevant legislation and regulations.

Anaesthesia is best done with the animal in a plastic bag and dropping in a small wad of cotton wool soaked in ether. Small mammals respire quickly and so the captive should be groggy enough to handle after a few seconds exposure to the vapours. Care should be taken to avoid the liquid ether coming into contact with the nose or lips of the animal (Twigg, 1975a). A way to avoid this would be to place the ether-soaked wad into a capped 35mm film canister with numerous holes drilled through and then dropping this into the bag. In cold environments it may be necessary to keep the ether warm as temperature controls the rate of ether vaporisation (Payne & Chamings, 1964). Lockie and Day (1964) describe a technique used for anaesthetising stoats *Mustela erminea* and weasels *M. nivalis* with ether. This was also used by Stoddart (1970) on water voles *Arvicola terrestris* who found that a 40-60 second dose was sufficient.

If anaesthesia is used it is important to release the captive only after the effects have worn off. An animal released in a 'woozy' state has a greatly reduced chance of survival. There is an argument against any use of anaesthesia due to the possible effects on survival. However Lockie and Day (1964) found no appreciable side effects which might have reduced survival of stoats and weasels even after anaesthetising individuals over 40 times. Stoddart (1970) also found no apparent harmful effects on water voles even though one animal was anaesthetised 36 times.

An additional reason for anaesthetising is that, in making the animal more tractable, it frees you from the medical caution of having to wear gloves. This is better for the animal as it increases the handler's sensitivity and dexterity and is also better for the human as (at least in warm climates) it is much more comfortable

Note that chloroform should not be used as this is highly toxic and results in many deaths (Twigg, 1975a). There is also the fact that it is carcinogenic to humans!

2.8.3 Holding an animal

Exactly how you hold the animal obviously depends on its size and weight, but most can be picked up by the scruff of the neck, using thumb and first finger (figure 1). This works well with smaller animals, but is inadvisable with animals over 200g. A more flexible grip is with the first and second finger inserted between jaw and shoulder (figure 2); this frees the thumb for manipulation, but should not be used if the animal is less than well anaesthetised. It is better for large animals.

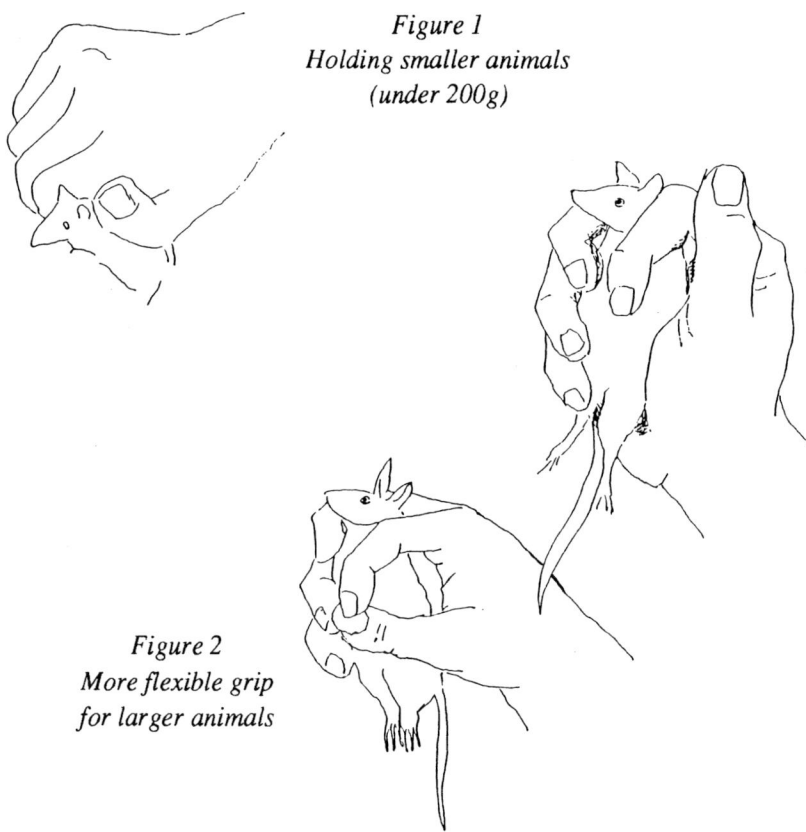

Figure 1
Holding smaller animals
(under 200g)

Figure 2
More flexible grip
for larger animals

Except with very small animals (or those with prehensile tails) it is bad practice to pick small mammals up by their tails (especially towards its tip). This can cause skin lesions and breakages to the vertebrae. Some species (e.g. the common Central and South American genus, *Proechimys*) have a natural point of weakness in the tail; normally used as a predator defence mechanism, it may leave you with a handful of twitching tail and a concussed rat on the floor.

There are some species which are undesirable to come into direct contact with (e.g. Norway rat *Rattus norvegicus*). An alternative to wearing surgical gloves would be to use a handling cone. The use of such cones may also negate the need to anaesthetise the captive. Hurst (1988) illustrates a cone used for holding house mice and le Boulenge-Nguyen & le Boulenge (1986) give a diagram of a cone used to hold small mammals while being ear tagged. Difficulties may arise when species of different sizes are being handled. Erickson (1947) describes a useful holder for such situations and Shadle & Ploss (1942) outline an adjustable cone used successfully for porcupines and beaver. With larger species it may be possible to use a simple cloth bag or pillow case. This method is successfully used by the UEA rabbit team, though in moments when concentration lapses there have been spectacular escapes! By manoeuvring the prisoner's nose into one corner examination can take place, including turning over for sexing etc. and ear tagging.

2.8.4 Marking animals

Marking is done so that the animal can be recognised again if it is recaptured. It is an integral part of capture-mark-recapture methodology and essential to many of the techniques used to estimate home range and movements of individual animals and densities of populations. Animal marking techniques can be split into two types: permanent and temporary. Some marking techniques, such as tissue removal, are regulated in the UK and it is worth checking for any relevant regulations in the host country prior to starting fieldwork.

2.8.4.1 Permanent marking

Techniques include ear tags (Le Boulenge-Nguyen & Le Boulenge, 1986; Scott, 1942; Stoddart, 1970; Twigg, 1975b), leg rings (Chitty, 1937; Twigg, 1975b), and tissue removal (Aldous, 1940; Twigg, 1975b, 1978). Stoddart (1970) successfully used small fish operculum tags after initial teething problems. With the exception of the technique of freeze marking (a technology which does not readily lend itself to the small expedition - see Franklin & El-Absy, 1985; Hurst, 1988), and spiny species where individual spines can be clipped (see Pigozzi, 1988), all permanent marking involves mutilation (either of the digits, tail or ears). The ethics of this are questionable, and it may well induce bias in the subsequent sampling. It can also most unpleasant to do.

Though theoretically these methods allow long term identification of individuals they are not without their associated problems. Fullagar & Jewell (1965) discusses the problems connected with the use of leg rings and Fairley (1982) and Montgomery (1985) examine their effect on recapture. In addition, in dense vegetation, it is likely that ear tags and leg rings will chafe and inhibit movement. Ear tags are known to have been ripped out and can cause increased tick infestation by 50 - 100% (Ostfeld *et al.*, 1993). The trauma caused by digit clipping and ear punching may have unknown effects on behaviour.

Recent developments in permanent marking include tattooing, transponders and the attachment of coloured pearls. A system for marking the toes of small mammals by tattooing with one to three dots (depending on size) using special ink has been developed (Poole, 1984). This has yet to be applied in the field but it has been used to successfully mark hundreds of laboratory mice. Transponders are inert microchips which are inserted sub-cutaneously and read using a special reader (Poole, 1994). Though costly the rejection rate is very low (usually due to faulty insertion) and have been used to tag newts (Fasola *et al.*, 1993), ground squirrels (Schooley *et al.*, 1993) among others (see Section 13.2.8). Salamon & Klettenheimer (1994) developed a technique using small plastic pearls. Though this techniques necessitates the use of anaesthetics they calculated that 9999 animals could be individually marked. They believe that the technique is at least as reliable as other ear tagging methods, without the disadvantage of snagging in vegetation.

2.8.4.2 Temporary marking

These techniques are probably sufficient for expedition use, depending on the length of time in a particular area. Temporary marking can be done at various levels of precision: clipping the animal's nails in a predetermined pattern (using, for example, right side for tens, left side for units), allows the most accurate identification (though there may be repercussions to the animals movement). Cutting away small patches of the outer coat to expose the underfur (which is almost always of a contrasting colour), is less precise but is a better "at a glance" method (though it does not work if the animal is wet). Gurnell & Flowerdew (1990) give an illustration of fur codes for small mammals. Such clips can remain visible for a few weeks to six months depending on the species.

Marking with dye or felt tip on fur or ears (e.g. Goldingay, 1986) is unsatisfactory except in the very short term as the material can be groomed off (it may also effect survivorship and so bias results). Rice-Oxley (1993) gives details for bleaching the tails of red squirrels *Sciurus vulgaris* which may be adapted, bearing in mind the possible effect on survivorship. Bleaching was also carried out on house mice *Mus domesticus* by Hurst (1988) The removal of the "pencil" (hairs projecting beyond the fleshy tip of the tail), is only partially useful as in many animals this part may have become naturally scuffed or damaged). Fluorescent pigments are also available (see Kaufman, 1989; Soderquist & Dickman, 1988), but of limited applicability in expedition work as they may wear off rapidly and may also cause increased susceptibility to predation.

2.8.5 Sexing animals
There are four ways in which small mammals may be sexed in the hand:
- body size and fur colour
- presence of testes
- status of nipples
- distance between urogenital openings

The first pair are not useful characters - between-sex differences in size and body weight (sexual dimorphism) are generally small and liable to a wide degree of overlap. Though a few species are sexually dimorphic for adult body size (Boonstra *et al.,* 1993; Ostfield & Heske, 1993) Sexual dichromism is almost unknown in eutherian small mammals (though it does occur in some marsupials - Flannery & Schouten, 1994).

In adult male rodents testes usually descend into the scrotal sacs only during the breeding season, at other times they recrudesce and are held abdominally. This can lead to confusion with juveniles (but see Sections 2.8.7 and 4.2.2).

Males have nipples too, though they are less well developed. Reproductively active adult females may be distinguished by the presence of milk and halos (see Section 2.8.6). Distance between openings is perhaps the best and most consistent criterion. The differences are illustrated in Corbet (1968) and Gurnell & Flowerdew (1990).

Some groups are difficult to sex without dissection. In some, notably shrews but also some marsupials, the testes remain in the body even when the males are sexually active (however see Searle, 1985). It is also worth remembering, when dealing with marsupials, that not all species have a pouch - e.g. *Metachirus nudicaudatus*.

2.8.6 Assessing reproductive condition

There are a number of techniques for dead specimens - these are described in Section 4.2.1, for living specimens this is best done by:

- males - presence of one or both testes in scrotal sacs and the size of the testes can give a clue to reproductive condition.
- females - presence of perforate vagina, presence of seminal plug in vagina, distended abdomen, presence of milk in nipples, presence of halos (bald areas around the nipples where the sucking action of feeding young has worn away the hair).

The greater number of characters in females allows a more precise determination of the stage that reproduction has reached. Recognising an imperforate vagina takes a little practice (try on laboratory mice before you leave). Seminal plugs do not occur in all species and are generally transitory. An obviously heavy and distended female is likely to be pregnant (if you palpate the abdomen do it with great tenderness).

In a lactating female a gentle squeeze on the nipples should produce a droplet of milk. Suckling babies wear away the fur from around the nipples, but the presence of such halos only means that the female has raised young recently, not that she definitely has any at the moment.

Descriptions of all the above can be also found in Gurnell & Flowerdew (1990).

2.8.7 Ageing of live animals

There are many techniques for determining relative and absolute age in dead animals (see Section 4.2.2). There are few reliable ones for short-term studies of living animals (King, 1991; Pucek & Lowe, 1975). Though slightly obscured for long-term studies by the problems of seasonal growth variation (e.g. Christensen, 1993; Leirs *et al.,* 1990; López-Fuster & Ventura, 1992), possibly the simplest is the division into the functional categories of young, juvenile and adult.

Apart from being much smaller, young animals often have proportionately larger paws and heads than adults (as puppies and kittens). The fur is often greyer and softer. Some of the down-like baby fur may still be present. In some species there are small balls of cartilage between the bones of the digits. These disappear with age, but while present give a slightly lumpy appearance. Areas of fur liable to abrasion (tail, ears) are often at their maximum cover at this time.

Juveniles are those animals which no longer resemble young in the proportion of their body parts but which are too small to be adults. Adults are those which are reproductively active or are the same size or weight as individuals which are.

Some authors have used length of the molar row as an age criterion (e.g. Provensal & Polop, 1993). Through studies of growth rates of captive animals, others (e.g. D'Andrea *et al.,* 1994) have related molar size classes to age. Though often quite accurate, such measurements can badly frighten the animal therefore should only be carried out with care and practice and not on rare species. For a useful bibliographical paper on age determination see Madsen (1967).

NOTE: once the animal has been processed it must be given time to recover. Transfer it to a separate (cloth) bag to let it do so. While this is happening bedding and box can be checked for faeces and ectoparasites. This is, perhaps, best done by tipping out the contents of the plastic bag onto a piece of white card (or a sheet of white plastic) and sorting through with forceps. Faecal pellets can be stored dry in a labelled, stoppered jar, and given further drying later if required. Ectoparasites are best picked up using a paintbrush dipped in alcohol and transferred to a labelled, stoppered bottle of 10% alcohol.

2.8.8 Procedures for use with snap traps

Data to record in the field note book is given in Section 2.7.3.

The capture should be tagged (with a tie-on label for preference) and a number written (in pencil) on the tag. Do not use a numbering system for each day. Keep a running system of collection numbers for the whole expedition (similarly do not divide up numbers between individual collectors, this can only add to confusion later on). Ideally each animal should have its own bag (confusion may otherwise result if tags come off).

2.8.9 Weights and measures

These are best taken back in camp if working on dead specimens, but done on site with live ones. Animals should be weighed and measured as soon as possible. You should bring with you a graded series of spring balances (see Section 13.1.2). Weights should be made to the nearest half gram (any greater accuracy is not needed and, considering the scale on spring balances, unlikely to be real).

The standard measurements are; length of tail, length of head and body (nose tip to tail base), length of hind foot (without claws), greatest length of ear. Additional measures (e.g. relative proportions of the parts of the limbs, whisker length, size of eye) may also prove useful (see below). Calculating body mass may be a useful alternative (Iskjaer et al., 1989) as weight on it's own may be subjective and liable to fluctuation even in the same individual.

When determining the length of the head & body and of the tail, it is best to use a pinboard. The animal is placed on this, and a pin placed by the root of the tail which is then stretched out. A second pin placed at the tailtip. The body is then pushed flat and straight and another pin inserted by the nose. The animal is removed and the distances measured.

The hind foot is best measured with callipers. Bending the foot at a right-angle to the leg ensures greater accuracy of measurement. If the toes are curled pinching or pressure should alter the tension on the tendons and result in their full flexion so that the hindfoot may be measured accurately. Always use the same hindfoot for measurements (that on the living animal's left is standard). Descriptions of measurement techniques can be found in Corbet (1968).

Biomechanical studies and work on body proportions is an interesting and neglected field. For information on the kind of additional measurements required, see Biknevicius (1993) and Miller & Anderson (1977).

2.8.10 Traps - to clean or not to clean?

Smell is very important to small mammals (see Hurst, 1989). If an animal has died in the trap (especially if blood has been shed), then it is best to clean the trap thoroughly (with alcohol if possible) before putting it back. However, there is a considerable body of literature on the wisdom or otherwise of cleaning traps that have successfully live-trapped (see reviews by Cox, 1989; Tew, 1987, and Hurst et al., 1994; Johnston & Jernigan, 1994; Palanza et al., 1994; and Rowe, 1970 as examples).

Most small mammals are odour-orientated and the smell of the opposite sex or just the same species can act as an attractant (Heske, 1987, Tew et al., 1994a). This may increase trap success. But, members of the same sex or different species may be discouraged (Cox, 1989; Hurst, 1989; Tew et al., 1994). Small mammals avoid the scents, scats or odour of their predators (Epple et al., 1993), so remove any such artefacts as soon as you become aware of them. If the problem persists - move your traps.

Gurnell & Flowerdew (1990) advocate the cleaning of traps when not in use and the lubrication of moving parts when necessary (except for the rotatory support of the spring wire on Longworths). The effect of different lubrication oils on trapping success of Longworth traps has been examined by Shore and Yalden (1991).

If trapping in little known areas you may wish to experiment to see which has the best effect. If in doubt clean out the traps and avoid a confounding variable in your analysis of results.

Section Three
SPECIMEN PREPARATION

3.1 How to kill an animal

It is messy and counter-productive to strangle or garotte specimens. Attempting to break the neck with a carefully placed blow or pressure is rarely successful. Whacking the animal against a hard surface is effective, but as a result the skull is often unserviceable as a museum specimen and other internal damage may make dissection unpleasant and/or unprofitable.

The best way is to over-anaesthetise. Put the animal in a sealed plastic bag with a wad soaked in ether (similar to Section 2.8.2). Use a tough bag and make sure it does not have any holes. For anything under 1kg five minutes should be enough but, if in doubt, replace the wad and go for a second dose (the stories about animals coming round while being dissected are true). From 1 to 2kg, an extra half-minute for every 100g is recommended.

3.2 Why to kill an animal

As discussed before, a combination of psychopathic compulsion and philatelic motivation should not be used to formulate a collecting policy. The only acceptable reasons for killing an animal on an expedition are:

- euthanasia of a "zombie" or otherwise damaged animal
- getting specimens for a medical project
- getting a voucher specimen to confirm identification or identify an unknown species
- getting specimens to enrich the collection of the host country.
- stomach content analysis

In the last two cases the expedition's "minimum collection" policy should be explained to the appropriate authorities in advance. This avoids disappointment and accusations of imperialist behaviour when showers of specimens are not forthcoming (see Section 11.1).

3.3 Skins

There are two ways to make skins: flat and round. The method you adopt will determine how you skin the animal. Flat skins are simpler to prepare, easier to store, less bulky to transport and are used by the Natural History Museum, London. Round skins make better study specimens and are used and recommended by many other institutions. It may be diplomatic to make a series of round specimens for the host country and a series of flat ones to be bought back to the UK.

Preparation of flat skins is described by Clevedon Brown & Stoddart (1977) and Corbet (1968). For the Preparation of round skins see references in Williams (1979). Corbet (1968) and Clevedon Brown & Stoddart (1977) are worth obtaining and taking to the field for reference. References to early literature (whose authors may well have been working in primative field condition similar to your expeditions' own) can be found in Booth (1944) who also gives methods for temporary preservation in the field. So that you do not botch your priceless specimen, it is recommended that laboratory rats and mice be used for pre-departure practice.

Morris & Wroot (1985) also provide a good guide to techniques of skinning mammals and how to preserve them. They also include useful guidance on how display them. This may be helpful if your project has an environmental education component.

NOTE: small animals are very much more difficult to skin than big ones. Animals that have been dead some time can be very difficult to skin, the skin may tear and the fur may come away very easily. Some species (e.g. *Lophuromys* from West Africa) have very thin skins and are naturally exceptionally difficult to skin easily. Making notes, during preliminary research, of any species where museum specimens persistently show tearing of the skin will alert you to this.

3.4 Skulls

You are more likely to get a firm identification from a skull than from a skin (though the work involved is correspondingly greater). Both Rosevear (1969) and Harrison (1972) provide a clear explanation of the anatomical terms associated with cranial morphology; you may find these helpful if you have to do identifications from skulls for yourself.

When cleaning skulls in the field it is not necessary to get off all the soft material. Museums generally have cleaning facilities (large tins full of the larvae of *Dermestes* beetles). These strip off the flesh and leave the skulls (and/or skeletons) perfectly clean (see Borell, 1938; Hall & Russell, 1933). However, hygiene (and the need to get things through customs) mean you should remove some of the soft parts immediately after dissection. Removing the brain, eyes, tongue and major cheek muscles may be enough. If you are too enthusiastic you can end up damaging the bone and features of taxonomic importance. The brain can be got out by macerating it with a needle inserted into the occipital foramen, and then sluicing out the mush with water from an un-needled syringe. Eyes and tongue can be removed with forceps, muscles pared away with a scalpel or with fine scissors. Do not boil the skulls as this softens up the cartilage that holds the bones together and makes them more likely to fall apart later (see Hooper, 1950). The use of meat tenderiser or papaya seeds has the same effect. If the flesh on the skull has dried out and is difficult to remove, soak in water before stripping off the flesh.

NOTE: when removing the cheek muscles, be careful not to damage the zygomatic arches. These are frequently important in identifying specimens.

Once the preliminary cleaning is done the skulls can be labelled (see Section 9.4) and then dried off. For this skulls should be placed in a sealed bag of very fine mesh muslin and hung in a light, airy, place (do not use a plastic bag as the resultant humid atmosphere encourages putrefaction - very densely woven material, old socks for example, are also unsuitable). This method keeps the skulls together, out of the way and avoids any problems with flies or other saprophages.

Once the skulls have dried out and the flesh fragments are firm and hard the skulls should be packed in sawdust or a similarly absorbent material. At this stage they may be safely sealed into containers. Skulls preserved in spirit tend to fall apart quickly, so they must be preserved dry.

If the area you are working in is very wet and you cannot air dry the skulls try putting them is small containers of sawdust (or a similarly absorbent material) and changing it frequently. Do not try putting the skulls by ant nests and getting the ants to clean them for you - they may dismember the skull and take the bits into the nest.

Clevedon Brown & Stoddart (1977) provide a general guide to the preparation of skulls.

NOTE: Skulls can also be used for ecological studies - especially if it is possible to infer niche differentiation from morphological characters (see Section 12).

3.5 Ectoparasites

With the odd exception (see Durden, 1991), the arthropods in the fur of small mammals are ectoparasites and fall into three main groups: fleas, lice and mites. Most suck blood, though some may feed on the dead skin of the animal. The ectoparasites are often species specific, sometimes several species will show resource partitioning on the host - each occurring on just one region of its body.

Many carry viral or bacterial diseases. Some can be fatal or debilitating (e.g. Lyme Disease, Typhus, Relapsing Fever, Encephalitis). So, even if you are not collecting them, it is a good idea to remove ectoparasites from any dead animals you are processing or live ones you are keeping for observation. If you do not get them, they may get you!

In the 1994 Zoological Record there were 35 papers describing one or more new species of parasites from mammals. Therefore your chances of making a new contribution are good.

First steps are the same whether for collecting for science or self-preservation; the arthropods are chloroformed (using ether, see Section 2.8.2) to death and then removed from the coat or skin of the specimen. This is best done with a soaked wad in a closed bag. If the animal is living then its head should remain outside the bag (the amount of anaesthetic it takes to put an animal under does not effect all ectoparasites). A live animal may be quickly combed out onto a piece of white paper (do it for too long and the animal may die of fright). More time can be spent on dead animals; the fur should be combed (the wrong way), particular attention being paid to the areas of the axillas, groin, tail base, genitalia and anus, behind the ears and under the chin. Closer searching may be done by lightly blowing the fur and picking it over with seekers. Get the parasites to drop onto a pale smooth surface (white card is best). They can then be picked up with the point of a paintbrush (moistened in alcohol or water), and transferred to a specimen bottle.

The ears often have mites attached - these are often very resistant to narcotization and may require direct application of a little neat alcohol (on the tip of a paint brush) to persuade them to let go. Whenever possible it is best to get mites out with the mouth parts intact, as these are important for their identification.

The nasal cavities may have unique species (see Smales *et al.,* 1990 as an example), but are difficult to examine in live specimens. If studying those of dead specimens, be careful not to damage the nasal bones of the skull as this will not enhance its latter value as a taxonomic artefact.

Small glass tubes with cork stoppers are the preferred receptacles. Separation of collections depends upon intent. Ideally, ectoparasites taken from each individual should be preserved separately (perhaps further divided by collections from dorsal and ventral parts). However, if this is not practical species or sexes can be grouped together. Under such circumstances it may be helpful to separate age-cohorts, sexes and individuals of the same species taken in different habitats or locations. All labels should be on uncoloured stiff paper/card and written in pencil. If a numbering system is used it should follow that used for field records and whatever skins and skulls are taken (see Section 9.4).

It may be useful to count how many ectoparasites are taken from each animal. This gives an idea of ectoparasite load. This can be related to the age and to the reproductive condition of the animal concerned and gives an insight into the animal's condition at the time of capture and hence how stressful to it was the overall environment. This can be particularly helpful in seasonal environments.

NOTE: Ectoparasites tend to stay with the host only as long as it is warm. If you find an animal dead in a live trap then check the bedding material for ectoparasites.

3.6 Preservation of the whole body

Arrangement of muscles and the form of the post-cranial skeleton are often useful for taxonomic studies, for mycological investigations and for functional ecology and morphology studies. It can therefore be helpful to preserve some carcasses in fluid for future reference. It may not be of direct benefit to you or the expedition, but can help 'science' in general.

For small animals simply slitting the stomach before immersing in alcohol is all that is needed. Evisceration should be considered. For larger animals you may also wish to inject the body with preservative (see references in Williams [1979]).

Some form of preservative bath is useful for an initial immersion of 48-72 hours. The Mammal Section at the Natural History Museum uses 85% ethyl alcohol as an ideal preservative, but in practice the choice is rather wider. The local distilled spirit has been frequently employed in this manner. This has the advantage of generally being quite cheap and easily available (but it may make your specimens smell funny). For guidance on preserving in liquid see Nagorsen & Peterson (1980).

Plastic jars can be used to preserve specimens while in camp, but specimens should be transferred to bags for travelling. If the specimens have been in fluid for more than a few days this will simply consist of wrapping the animal up in a sealed plastic bag (those with the snap together seals are best) It may be worth double bagging, with one label with the specimen and one label in the second bag. For fresher animals, stuffing the body cavity with preservative soaked wadding is recommended.

NOTE: when moving specimens from one medium to another, always check that the labels are in good condition. Replace any that are not.

3.7 Moult

Moult status is a standard piece of information and is usually included the pecimen label in diagrammatic form (see Clevedon Brown & Stoddart, 1977; & Corbet, 1968). It can provide an estimation of relative age (Ecke & Kinney, 1956), and can be an important clarifier in species where seasonal polychromism has caused taxonomic problems, or when attempts are being made to assess reproductive status (some species have halos which persist after suckling has finished and the halos only disappear at moult time when the new hair grows through).

Areas of moult activity on a skin are indicated by the dark spots or patches of melanin, visible when the skin is removed from the body and interior examined. For examples of technique and application, and for interpretation of data see Antúnez *et al.,* (1990), Ecke & Kinney (1956), Kryltzov (1964) and Ventura (1992).

3.8 Condition

Body mass and fat deposits give an indication of the level of nutritional stress the survey population is currently under. This can be useful for species with cyclic densities or in strong seasonal environments. For techniques see Angerbjorn (1986), Bailey (1968), Brochu *et al.,* (1988) and Krebs & Singleton (1993).

Section Four
WORKING ON THE SPECIMEN

4.1 How to dissect

4.1.1 Tools of the trade
Not a great deal of equipment is needed. The following should suffice: 1 pair of fine scissors, 1 pair of heavy scissors, 2 scalpels (different handle sizes), scalpel blades of the following sizes 10, 10A, 15 and 20 and two pairs of forceps (one big, one small). For suppliers see Section 13.1.4 and 13.2.4.

4.1.2 Medical precautions
Blood may aerosol into fine droplets as vessels are cut, unpleasant blood-born diseases are to be found in small mammals (particularly rodents - e.g. lassa fever from blood, Q fever from the placenta). It is therefore wise to wear a mask when dissecting (even if it does get hot and sticky in a warm climate). Cuts in fingers are an added danger. If the small mammal community you are working with contains particularly well-known public health dangers (e.g. in West Africa, *Mastomys natalensis*), then wear gloves too (the disposable latex sort are most convenient).

4.1.3 What to do
You are not doing a dissection for an exam, so looks do not need to count a great deal. Just open the body cavity with a small cut to the middle of the belly of the skinned corpse where it is being held taut by a pair of forceps. Blood must be sluiced away. Never leave a dissection part done as flies are likely to get at it (the results can be unpleasant). Before starting you may find that the body has gone rigid through rigor mortis. This can be removed by rubbing the body lightly between the hands or by lightly manipulating it (as one would a foot with cramp).

4.1.4 Disposal of corpses
Dissected corpses can either be buried or burnt. The latter is preferred as burying can attract scavengers. Alternatively, if not rotten, the meat used for bait on further traps.

4.2 What to collect - which bits, why and how
Not all parts will yield data of scientific interest. The main body parts of interest are the reproductive tracts, eye lens' (age determination), body fluids, body tissues, guts and faeces. Each is dealt with in greater detail below. Each

can be used for a very different purpose. The potential data set from each animal is immense.

4.2.1 Reproduction

Outside Europe and North America, data on reproduction in small mammals is often very sparse. The data you collect can be of great value, not only for the greater knowledge of a species' natural history but because in strongly seasonal environments patterning of small mammal reproduction can give clues to the periodicity of events in the community as a whole (see Barnett & da Cunha, 1994 and references therein, and Breed, 1992; Feldhammer *et al.,* 1993; Fisher, 1991; Henry, 1994; Kerle & Howe, 1992)

From females, useful data from embryos includes: the size (greatest length), weight (with and without placenta), developmental state (e.g. state of limb formation, development of eyes and of fur), number of embryos (written as n + n, and referring to the number in the left and right uterine horns, respectively). The presence of embryos in the process of reabsorption is also of interest.

Dewsbury *et al.,* (1977) give methods for studying oestrus cycles in rodents. Negus *et al.,* (1977) provides an example of the data to be got in this type of study.

From males, the size and weight of the testes is of interest. Presence of uterine scars will reveal if the female had given birth before. Examination of seminiferous vesicles will reveal sperm activity in males. However, both these data points require microscopical examination and may best be done later in the lab. Techniques of preservation are given in Clevedon Brown & Stoddart (1977) and Corbet (1968).

4.2.2 Absolute ageing of animals

A useful bibliographic reference on age determination is Madsen (1967).

4.2.2.1 Weight

In some cases it is possible to make the age-size relationships quite sophisticated - using equations that account for the allometric growth of the various body parts (see Jeanmaire-Besancon, 1986; de Paz, 1986). Simple characters such as weight are not very reliable determinators of age (see Fuller, 1988; Viitela, 1989), though may have to do in expedition circumstances. If possible other, more reliable methods should be employed (though don't worry if you haven't the time or the methodology to do them - you may not need the precision they give for your studies).

4.2.2.2 Teeth

Teeth can be good indicators of age. The molars have a pattern of ridges and troughs which, apart from having great taxonomic significance, can be used to age animals as the wear on the teeth can be divided into age-related classes depending on what features appear (or disappear) over time. The only disadvantage is that this technique requires a large sample size because of individual variation in wear patterns (mostly due to variation in the erosive abilities of diet). This can be gained in advance for common species with the use of museum collections (a large sample size being in excess of two hundred animals - see Adamczewska-Andrzejewska, 1971, 1973). Stages of tooth eruption can also be used to assess developmental stage. For an example of use of tooth criteria in tropical field studies see Atramentowicz (1986).

4.2.2.3 Eye lens weight

First reported by Leopold & Calkins (1951) and Lord (1959), this technique relies on the observation that the weight of the eye lens increases incrementally over age, with little variation within an age-cohort (see Andersen & Jensen, 1972). It is a widely used and reliable measure (see Askaner & Hansson, 1970; Hagen *et al.*, 1980; Hardy *et al.*, 1983). But the rates vary widely between species and calibration needs to be done anew for a new species. If longer-term population studies are being done then this is a very useful technique. Statistical treatments are given by Hagen *et al.*, (1980). Teska & Pinder (1986) have shown that the relationship of eye lens weight to age is not always a simple primary one, but that it can be influenced by diet.

4.2.2.4 Cranial studies

For some species, the age-related changes in cranial proportions are known from studies of captive specimens (e.g. Quéré *et al.*, 1994), providing an absolute rather than relative measure of age. While applicable to wild populations, this only works with clean skulls and cannot be done on living animals.

4.2.3 Tissue and fluid samples

Apart from the whole body (see Section 3.6), the main parts that can be taken are: the heart, the liver and the kidneys.

The point of taking these is generally for later analysis of proteins by electrophoresis or by analysis of DNA or chromosomes. While very useful (e.g. Hogan *et al.*, 1993 and Wócjcik, 1993), such techniques are sophisticated and time consuming. It is vital that the material be prevented from decaying for, as soon as proteins begin to break up into smaller fragments, the definition of the data is reduced. The specialist cryogenic preservation techniques required to avoid this involve equipment that is heavy and expensive. It is only worth collecting the material if you have been asked to do so or will be doing later work yourself. Techniques are reviewed by Sherwin (1991).

4.2.4 Guts and intestines

Analysis of the relative proportions and volumes of the various parts of the alimentary canal can give information on diet (see Section 5), water relations and digestive strategy as can analysis of their morphology (see Barry, 1977; Emmons, 1981; Freudenberger, 1992; Hume *et al.,* 1993; Myrcha, 1964; Osawa & Woodall, 1992a,b; Perrin & Curtis, 1980; Snipes & Kriete, 1991; Tedman & Hall, 1985; for examples and Schiek & Millar, 1985 for review).

Mucosal surface area of the stomach and the morphology of the villi also have functional relations (see Barry, 1976; Perrin & Curtis, 1980). Though seasonal (e.g. Osawa & Woodall, 1990, 1992b) changes or changes in relation to diet quality (e.g. Hofmann, 1983) may obscure things a little.

Barry (1976) provides methods for calculating the surface area of the small intestine. Barry (1977) does the same for the ceacum and colon rectum.

Relative proportions should be measured while the guts are fresh. Solutions for the preservation of intestines are given in Clevedon Brown & Stoddart (1977) and Corbet (1968). Techniques of preparation for anatomical study appear in Schiek & Millar (1985) and references therein.

4.2.5 Faeces

In addition to collecting faeces from the external environment, additional samples may be obtained from the colon of the dead animal. You may wish to label such specimens separately as they can be useful in the determination of bias via differential digestibility of foodstuffs (see Section 5). Material is best preserved dried. Laying out on absorbent paper or sun-drying is adequate. Make sure to keep samples separate during this process. Putman (1984) gives an overview of methodology and the kind of data obtainable from faeces.

4.2.6 Endoparasites

Specificity is just as great as in ectoparasites. The rationale behind the study is similar (see Section 3.5). A good review of the topic and introduction to techniques can be found in *Mammal Review* (parts 2 and 3, Volume 17, 1987), which contains ten papers on endoparasites of small mammals. Smales *et al.,* (1990) provide a nice example of a thorough endoparasitological examination.

4.2.7 Blood

Studies of blood are useful for parasitological studies and for providing materials for electrophoretic studies. Samples may be drawn from the veins of the ears or tail or from the tip of the tail. It is also supposed to be possible to get a sample from the blood vessels just behind the eye. Such sampling techniques are best practised before departure, under supervision, on laboratory animals. Gardner *et al.,* (1987) provide an introduction to techniques.

4.2.8 Others

According to Kutuzov & Sicher (1952), the anatomy of the palate may give a clue to diet and mode of feeding. These authors also give instructions for techniques of preparation and the anatomical terminology required.

Section Five
DIETARY ANALYSIS

Although it is possible to work out what has been eaten by animals from tooth marks on food remains (see Lawrence & Brown, 1973), this does not give a very satisfactory insight. It may be impossible to do in places where the small mammals fauna is not well known. Two of the best ways of getting to know the diet of the animals are to look at faecal matter and at gut contents. For a review of the techniques available for faecal analysis see Putman (1984).

The techniques applied depend on the intended depth of the study. For a little known fauna it may be sufficient to simply classify into broad categorise (fruit, leaves, insects, vertebrate remains etc). Delany (1972) gives examples of this kind of approach for tropical Africa, McPhee (1988) does the same for Papua New Guinea. As this data is of the 'snap shot' variety, the utility of more detailed investigations is probably compromised by the short stay of most expeditions. However, it may be possible to build with data gathered over several visits.

Techniques in micro-analysis of gut contents, whereby samples of the contents are mounted on permanent slides and components identified by comparison to a reference collection, are described by Hansson (1970). Though this is not always the case (see Williams, 1962), such analysis is often quantified (e.g. Gebczynska & Myrcha, 1966; Zubaid & Gorman, 1991). The three commonest techniques are i) frequency of occurrence, ii) the number and, iii) the area covered by different fragment types. The method used will effect statistical accuracy, Norbury (1988a) provides a useful comparison of the three techniques. Other useful reviews of the methodology include Loeb & Schwab (1989) and Norbury & Sanson (1992).

Faecal analysis techniques are given by Bhadresa (1977; 1981; 1987), Hearney & Jennings (1983) and by Norbury (1988b). Examples of gut analysis are given by Gebczynska & Myrcha (1966), Hamilton (1941), Myers & Vaughan (1964), Rathbun (1979), Williams (1962), and Zubaid & Gorman (1991). If you want to try the faecal technique out before departure, see the techniques, recommendations and keys in Bhadresa (1981), which lets you try the whole thing out on rabbit pellets.

Generally, such techniques are can only be deployed if you have access to a good field lab or if you bring the material back with you to work on. This may be the most practical, especially as field time is normally precious. Stomachs and guts can either be preserved whole (Hamilton, 1941; Williams, 1962), or the contents removed and preserved (Rathbun, 1979; Zubaid &

Gorman, 1991) (see Nagorsen & Peterson, 1980 for stomach preservation techniques). Faecal matter can either be dried or stored in preservative, though the environment may dictate which method is most suitable.

The actual analysis is time consuming and tedious and requires a reference collection of foodstuffs. Both the collection and preparation of these may cause problems for expeditions working in remote areas. For studies of the diet of herbivorous species, a set of microscope slides of the epidermis of (normally) the leaves is required. Methods for making such slides often include the chemical maceration of plant leaves and can be fiddley. An alternative and novel approach is presented by Jennings (1979) and was used by Hearney & Jennings (1983). It should be possible to make microscope slides from dried plant specimens (reducing the need to carry chemicals etc into the field) though this would be worth checking during pre-expedition planning. For insectivorous and carnivorous species a collection of all relevant prey species will need to be included in the expedition's aims. (Not all bits are needed: for carnivores perhaps just skull mandibles and fur of prey species, arthropod jaws, wings and sclerites for insectivores).

You may at least be able to work out how many different kinds of plants the animal had eaten (see Williams, 1962; Zubaid & Gorman, 1991). To do a really thorough job you should also be determining not only what the animals are eating (difficult enough as we have seen), but assessing 'selectivity' ie comparing the relative frequency of the items in the gut with those in the field. A suitable methodology is provided by Myers & Vaughan (1964). You would probably need the co-operation of botanical and entomological colleagues to achieve this.

One of the problems bedevilling such studies is that of differential digestibility of the food items. This means that some elements will be over-represented in the sample (see Batzli & Cole, 1979; Hamilton, 1941). Without investigative lab work there is not a great deal you can do about this.

Be careful of inter-technique variability, Loeb & Schwab (1989) compare three methods for determining diet quality. These samples can differ in the apparent proportion of materials (see Norbury, 1988b). Therefore be careful if the analysis includes comparing data obtained using different methods. It may be worth analysing both faecal and stomach contents.

Whilst some small mammals are known to be specialist nectivores, acting as pollinators for the plants they visit (e.g. honey possums *Tarsipes*, Vose, 1973; Wiens *et al.,* 1979), it is becoming increasingly apparent that other species of small mammal which lack obvious morphological specialisation's for nectivery or pollen eating, may also visit flowers and be important as pollinators (see Coe & Isaac, 1965; Janson *et al.,* 1981; Lumer, 1980; Steiner, 1981, Wiens & Rourke, 1978; Wiens *et al.,* 1983 for examples and Kress *et al.,* 1994 for an overview). Consequently do check your specimens (especially arboreal and scansorial ones) for pollen on the fur, especially around the snout, lips, whiskers and chest. Any such pollen found should be preserved for later identification (see Beattie, 1971 for techniques).

Section Six
TRACKING SMALL MAMMALS

In addition to standard trapping studies the examination of small mammals movement, home range and activity is of great interest. There are several techniques for this all of which have their positive and negative aspects. The following papers compare techniques: Bergstrom (1988), Desy *et al.*, (1989) and Jones (1983) (radio tracking and grid trapping), Jike *et al.*, (1988) and Mullican (1988) (radio tracking and powder tracking), Johns (1979) (trapping, marker bait and smoked plate tracking).

6.1 Grid trapping

This is probably the most practical method of studying the movement distribution and home range of small mammals on expeditions. Gurnell & Flowerdew (1990) give details of using trapping to determine home range, movement indices and distribution. Be aware that the data obtained is 'trap-revealed' and may not show a true picture. Placing bait in traps will possibly skew results as it actively attracts individuals. Gurnell & Flowerdew (1990) discuss this technique in more detail.

Do not be put off by the negative aspects of this tracking method. If the species under investigation is poorly known any information is of value. There are problems associated with all the tracking techniques and if organised this should require less additional time and effort. Hawes (1977) used grid trapping to calculate the home range and territoriality of two shrew species and Stoddart (1970) studied the range, dispersion and dispersal of water voles *Arvicola terrestris*. Davis (1953) discusses ways of analysing home ranges from recapture data.

6.2 Radio tracking

This is probably the most 'sexy' of the tracking techniques, possibly because it introduces high technology (electronic beeping boxes) to a field science that otherwise relies on fairly basic equipment. It is often perceived as the answer to all the questions and problems of studying wild animals in the field. Unfortunately this is not the case and failure to take into account its drawbacks and pitfalls can be costly in both time and money. Having said this the data collected can be very exciting as it allows the remote study of species. Such data may be unobtainable to such accuracy (without disturbance) by any other means. Radio tracking is most often used to study home range, dispersal, habitat utilisation and activity patterns.

When planning a project involving radio tracking you need to consider the method of data collection (Harris *et al.,* 1990), fix accuracy (Springer, 1979; Lee *et al.,* 1985; Saltz & Alkon, 1985; White & Garrot 1986), home range asymptotes and sample size (Harris *et al.,* 1990) and autocorrelation of data (Swihart & Slade, 1985) among others.

One basic requirement is to know where you are so you can fix the position of the animal being tracked and subsequently plot it for analysis. Researchers have tackled this in a variety of ways including placing out a fixed grid of markers (Sanderson & Sanderson, 1964; Morris & Hoodless, 1992), lying out a set of parrallel wires marked at 5m intervals (Bright & Morris, 1991; 1992) and cutting a grid of paths (Fitzgibbon & Rathbun, 1994). If you are certain of your position you then can find the animals position in relation to you. This can be done by using two or more compass bearings to obtain a fix (Bowen, 1982; Heezen & Tester, 1967; Loft *et al.,* 1984), by using direction and signal strength (Douglass, 1989), by using an automated system (French *et al.,* 1992) or locating by sight and directly plotting on a map (Bright & Morris, 1991, 1992; Kolb, 1991; Morris, 1988; Stallings *et al.,* 1994). This latter method can cause disturbance and may not be practical with small mammals in thick undergrowth, though Bright & Morris (1991; 1992) found no apparent disturbance. Note that if you have an animal that has a small home range and your fixes are not too accurate you may find your animal hardly moves!

Radio tracking equipment is not cheap, collars suitable for small mammals, depending on the size of the species to be studied, range from £66 - £100+ (late 1994 prices). Receivers cost £390 upwards, and you need headphones, antenna etc. Tag size is dependant on animal size and as a consequence so is battery life span. Lifespan can vary from one week to ten plus weeks, hence the radio tracking study needs to be planned accordingly. Take as much advice as possible and become familiar with the techniques you will be using. It takes time to learn and practice prior to the expedition will be time well spent. For advice and equipment in the UK Biotrack and Mariner Radar are very helpful (see Sections 13.1.9 and 13.2.8).

A good introduction to radio tracking and analysis is given by Kenward (1987) and Harris *et al.,* (1990) is invaluable when planning a project. White & Garrott (1990) give 383 pages of information on radio tracking data analysis and there are computer programmes available (see Sections 13.1.9 and 13.2.8). Examples of small mammal studies using radio tracking are: Douglass (1989), Fitzgibbon & Rathbun (1994), Jones (1989), Morris & Hoodless (1992), Sanderson & Sanderson (1964), Smith *et al.,* (1993),

Stallings *et al.,* (1994) and Wolton (1985). Lenders *et al.,* (1986) provide an interesting approach, thermo-sensitive radiotelemetry.

The presence of antenna and a beeping box of electronic equipment may cause suspicion in some countries, particularly near military zones. Check whether you require permission to use radio tracking equipment, it may take some time to obtain. Under such circumstances do not go out into the field without your letter of authorisation.

6.3 Transponder tracking

Originally developed for individually marking laboratory animals and pets (see Section 2.8.4.1), these inert Transponders have recently been used to track rats in a farmyard. A grid of readers was set up connected to automatic data loggers. It was then possible to follow the activity and movements of individual rats fitted with transponders. They have also been used to record the frequency and duration of nest visits by parent birds (see Section 13.2.8 for equipment manufacturers).

This method does not produce as accurate data as radio tracking as it relies on tagged individuals in coming within range of the readers. It does have the advantage of being automatic once set up. In addition the transponder microchips cost only a few pounds which is going to be less painful to the pocket if the study animals get eaten! However this needs to be weighed up against the cost of the readers which range from £400 - £750.

6.4 Spool-and-line tracking

A direct way of tracking animals has been described by Miles *et al.,* (1981). Here a metal spool, with single-strand terylene thread wound around it, was attached to the body of the study animal. The free end of the thread was held by the investigator and the animal followed through the forest. The spool stayed attached for around five days. During this time behaviour appeared to be normal. Home ranges could be determined and sleeping places marked.

This technique, since it leaves a record of the animal's passage through the forest, could be used as a remote method of indirectly observing an animals daily activities. It has obvious potential, but appears to have been little exploited. Anderson *et al.,* (1988), Berry *et al.,* (1987) and Miles *et al.,* (1981) have all successfully used this technique. Hawkins & Macdonald (1992) applied this technique to badgers *Meles meles* and discuss some of its associated problems.

6.5 Powder tracking

Powder tracking involves dusting captured animals with fluorescent ultraviolet reflective pigment (see Section 13.2.8). This is done by putting the animal in a bag containing a small amount of powder and gently shaking. Once released the subsequent trail can be followed and mapped using an ultraviolet lamp (Jike *et al.,* 1988; Lemen & Freeman, 1985; Mullican, 1988).

This is a relatively simple and cheap technique but the powder can wear off fairly rapidly, Lemen & Freeman (1985) found that tracks were only left the first night. Apparently some researchers filled a small sack with powder and tied this to the tail base of kangaroo rats, a slit in the bag allowed a small amount of powder to be deposited on each 'hop'. This meant the powder lasted for longer. Kaufman (1989) in another novel approach used fluorescent powders to study social interactions of rodents.

Like spool-and-line tracking there is no timescale and it is only useful in dry environments. It should only be used on nocturnal species, the appearance of a brightly coloured animal during the day is likely to be noticed by predators! Worries have been expressed about the possible adverse effects of using this powder on small mammals. Stapp *et al.,* (1994) found few significant pathological effects, but recommended the minimisation of exposure of study animal respiratory tissue to large doses of such powder.

6.6 Other techniques

Several other techniques for tracking animals have been developed, although they are less favoured since the advent of radio tracking. However, they may be of use to expeditions and therefore are briefly outlined below.

The use of radio-active tracers is quite an old technique in the field study of small mammal behaviour (see references in Woods & Mead-Briggs, 1978). It can be very useful for burrowing animals or those which spend a long time underground. Wolton (1985) used the radioactive marking of faeces to examine range marking in the wood mouse *Apodemus sylvaticus.* The major problem, apart from the delicacy of some of the equipment, is likely to be the attitude of airlines and customs to the material being transported.

Natural or artificially obtained footprints can be very useful for tracking animals, especially if they have been toe-clipped. Justice (1961) developed a method using a grid of smoked kymograph paper protected from the elements by milk cartons. This method has been adopted and modified by several other researchers including Bailey (1968), Brown (1966), Johns (1979) and Martin (1972). An alternative technique using ink pads and blotters was developed by Lord *et al.,* (1970), Flowerdew (1976) recommends an improvement to this technique. To avoid the spoiling of track records Taylor (1973) developed a device which would change the recording surface. It would also be possible to use powdered-slides (Boonstra *et al.*, 1992) and sand trays (Bider, 1968) as tracking surfaces. To bait, or not bait, tracking stations will be a matter of experimentation as both have been carried out with success (Flowerdew, 1976).

Tracking without toe-clipping has been carried out by Erlinge (1967) on otters and on shrews by Doucet & Bider (1974). However with unknown species present this is unlikely to be possible on an expedition.

The use of marker bait (bait loaded with coloured woollen/nylon fibres) is also a technique worth consideration. Marked bait is fed to animals and then the distribution of marked faeces in a grid of shelters is recorded (Johns, 1979; Randolph, 1973). The drawback with this technique is that to feed sufficient marked bait it is necessary to hold the animal in captivity for a period of time (over night) which may effect its behaviour and territory. It also requires the expedition to have facilities for holding animals in captivity (see Section 7.12).

Section Seven
OTHER TECHNIQUES

There are many other techniques which may be used instead of, or as a compliment to, trapping. Lack of space prevents the list below from embracing a wider selection, but it may provide some useful jumping-off points.

7.1 Owl pellets

Owls normally swallow their prey whole. The flesh is digested off and then the bones, skull and fur are regurgitated. Birds of prey also produce pellets but, because they tend to decapitate their prey, their pellets often do not contain the skulls of their prey. This can hinder the process of identification. The use of pellets to a mammal survey is that owls can find species that field workers (and their traps) may miss. Indeed there are several small mammal species that are known only from remains taken from owl pellets (Nowak, 1991a,b). Anderson & Long (1961) used owl pellets to compliment trapping in their study of Mexican small mammals.

The pellets can be teased apart (wet or dry, by hand or with forceps) and the mammal remains laid aside. In the UK identification of material from owl pellets is fairly simple as the mammal fauna is quite small and very well known (see Yalden & Morris, 1990). This is not the case in the tropics. It may be best to wait and work on collected pellets once back in UK where comparative materials are available in museum collections. Identification of remains can be quite tricky since not only the size but the proportions of the bones can change through age (see Yalden & Morris, 1990 for examples with the British mammal fauna). Draulans *et al.*, (1987) describe techniques for the identification of small mammal remains from grey heron pellets. It is sometimes possible to distinguish sexes on the basis of bones alone (Ventura, 1993)

Pellets will not necessarily give a representative indication of the composition of the small mammal community of an area. As Jaksic & Yanez (1979) have pointed out, owl pellet samples have a distinct bias towards species that have primarily nocturnal activity patterns. In addition, Dickman *et al.*, (1991) have shown that there are bias's within species too. They have shown that owls preferentially hunt specific size and age classes and that there can also be a sex-bias in the samples from owl pellets.

7.2 Carnivore scats

These are generally of less use than owl pellets as the animal tends to have been fairly well masticated before the remains were excreted. Sufficient fragments may survive to provide positive identifications (see Baker & Degabriele, 1987; Brown & Triggs, 1990; Brunner & Wallis, 1986; Wallis & Brunner, 1987). Nevertheless the difficulties of conducting identifications of fragmentary parts from an imperfectly-known fauna remain. It may be possible to identify prey remains from fur as well as skeletal remains (see Brunner *et al.*, 1976; Friend, 1978). But this needs a reference collection if it is to be of any use (see Section 7.5).

As with owl pellets it is probably best to retain specimens and work them up when a good comparative collection is available (in addition to that made during the course of the fieldwork). Putman (1984) discusses the problems of estimating the proportion of prey items in carnivore scats. Mukherjee *et al.*, (1994) gives a technique for the standardisation of scat analysis.

7.3 Dental impressions

In some groups (e.g. *Microorrzomys*), separation of species on the basis of external characters of pelage and measurements is difficult. Skull and dental characters may be the only alternative. Dental impressions offer a way to avoid killing large numbers of animals. The technique was developed by a conservation-minded bat worker, Fif Robinson, and is fully described in his paper (Robinson, 1989). Though not yet widely applied to small mammals the transition should be possible. A reference collection, made from skulls in a museum collection, is a prerequisite for successful operation of this technique in the field, as is a familiarity with the taxonomic literature to allow the salient features of dental morphology to be noticed and identified. The extra work involved is amply repaid by the reduction of futile killing.

7.4 Sand trays

In the UK it is possible to identify small mammals from the paw impressions (e.g. Lawrence & Brown, 1973). However, it is not so easy in the tropics where the faunas are less well known. Even if used where the knowledge of the small mammal community is great sand trays are unlikely to tell you exactly what has been there. They are best used as indicators of levels of activity and as indicators of where activity is happening. In this context they can be valuable in determining where to put traps if a number of alternative holes or sites are available (see Section 2.3.2).

7.5 Fur pipes

An additional test of activity is the fur pipe. A narrow piece of rigid tubing or pipe, into which double-backed Sellotape or small (blunt) pins have been attached to face downwards and inwards from above. Any animal passing through the pipe will, if big enough, leave a bit of fur on the impediment. This can later be retrieved and compared with a reference collection.

Fur pipes can also be used to determine the best place for traps (useful if trap numbers are limited and a certain amount of scouting out has to be done in advance). Scotts & Craig (1988) detected the presence of a rare species missed during normal live trapping.

They may be baited or left unbaited. Scotts & Craig (1988) describe a simple, but elegant, fur pipe that can be hand-made from commercially available PVC components. This design retains the bait allowing a longer 'active' life-span. Suckling (1978) gives a design used to detect small mammals in trees.

The advantage for compiling species inventories is that they don't require the same effort as trapping and can be left unattended for long periods of time. However this is balanced by the processing time required in the lab. A key of hairs is needed to carry out identification which can cause problems if unexpected or new species crop-up. It may be possible to compile this from museum specimens. Teerink (1991) gives details of hair structure and key preparation as well as an identification key of some 73 West-European mammals. For Australian mammals see Brunner & Coman (1974).

7.6 Ultra-sonic detectors

Bats are not the only small mammals to make ultra-sonic noises. Though perhaps commonest in mother-infant interactions, ultra-sonic calls are also used by adult rodents and shrews (Sewell, 1968). These can be detected by the same kind of basic ultra-sonic detectors commonly used by bat workers in the UK (see Mitchell-Jones, 1987). These can detect areas of greatest activity and be useful in locating suitable places for positioning traps.

7.7 Nightlighting

Nightlighting is not used very frequently in small mammal studies. Emmons (1984) reported good results in various parts of the Amazon as did McCabe & Elison (1986) in North America. However, the technique is very obviously dependent on a good system of existing trails, familiarity with the habitat and the habits of the animals within it, and the ability to identify them. It is also very prone to inter-observer bias. Under anything less than exceptional circumstances it is suggested that this system is likely to frighten off more than is seen. Though it may be useful for confirming the existence of nocturnal mammals too large to fit into the traps, under the circumstances most expeditions find themselves in, the results are unlikely to balance the time spent.

7.8 Luminous tags

Such tags have been used to follow larger mammals at night. They come in sizes appropriate for small mammals, and stay on long enough to be worked on by an expedition. They are easy to attach, do not harm the animal and can be seen at a distance (though not in very dense undergrowth). They allow individual animals to be followed (though little more can be achieved without supplemental lighting). They are, perhaps, better suited to long-term fieldwork than to the short-term work of expeditions.

Morris (1988) used luminous tags to aid the location of hedgehogs while radio tracking and Rathbun (1979) used beta lights to study elephant shrews.

7.9 Nests

Use of radio tracking and spool-and-line techniques could lead to the discovery of resting places and nests. These are normally very difficult to discover. Direct searches for nests are possible (though time consuming) and can result in valuable information (see Heim de Balsac & Hutterer, 1982). Studies of nests, useful in itself since so very few are described (see Mares & Genoways, 1982), can also yield information on ectoparasites, litter size and timing of reproduction.

If nests are particularly obvious it may be possible to use them as an index of density and distribution. This has been done with *Rhynchocyon* elephant shrews (Fitzgibbon & Rathbun, 1994) and successfully used by the Oxford University Njule '92 expedition (Hanna & Anderson, 1993).

7.10 Interviews with local people

Talking to local people can tap a rich vein of information. It is possible to get data on animals you may have missed, seasonal and annual fluctuations in density, local names (and the reasons for them), local myths and legends and local taboos (good for lectures and may help for conservation). It may be unwise to use formal interview format as it may put people off. Never pry and try and keep your session short. Always explain why you are asking the questions (rural people are often very suspicious of anything that smacks of officialdom - you might be a tax collector in disguise). Double check your information - some people may not realise what weight you are putting on their information and fabricate tales. Photographs (some of expected animals, others of some from another continent) are a good test of the reliability of a source.

Don't forget (if decorum allows it) to question both male and female members of the population (recently two French ornithologists, searching remote regions of Madagascar for the slender-billed flufftail, had almost lost hope as all the hunters they asked denied that the bird existed. They finally asked the women who, it turned out, knew the bird very well. The reason? The slender-billed flufftail is a marsh dweller. Only women go to the marshes to collect reeds for matting and basketry - the men never visit the marshes and restrict their hunting activities to the forest). For guidance and techniques for this type of work see Bellamy (1992) and Kapila & Lyon (1994).

The local cat population represents another local source of data. Like the owls (see Section 7.1) they may catch specimens that you missed. The most famous example of this comes from Stephens Island, a rocky outcrop off the northern coast of South Island, New Zealand. The entire population of this island's endemic wren, *Xenicus lyalli*, was exterminated by the lighthouse keeper's cat. All sixteen known specimens were also 'collected' by this animal. Ornithologists had otherwise been unaware of this bird.

7.11 Middens
In rural communities refuse is often dumped on a communal midden. This can be a rich source of material for the dedicated mammalogist since skulls and other material can often be found there. This may give an insight into local hunting practices that could not be obtained by other means. It is unlikely to be of much use for the smaller mammals, however, since their bones and skulls are crushed and dispersed relatively easily. It has, however, been used with some success on larger mammals.

7.12 Keeping animals in captivity
This can be very rewarding if done well, but remember that the animal's welfare comes before scientific curiosity. Only keep a specimen if you have the conditions under which it will behave naturally (otherwise there is little point in keeping it in the first place). Studies of captive animals can allow you to observe feeding behaviour and test food preferences and capabilities (see Kostelecka-Myrcha & Myrcha, 1964a,b; Murua *et al.,* 1980). You may even be able to test social interactions (e.g. Gurnell, 1977). It is also an opportunity

to obtain samples for pellet identification (see Section 7.13) and for identification of fur from fur-pipes (see Section 7.5).

Remember to avoid taking pregnant or lactating females. Don't put animals of different sizes in the same cage - or you may end up with just one much fatter one in the morning. After your observations, try to release the animal as close to the place you found it as possible. Churchfield (1990) gives some advice for keeping shrews in captivity. It may be wise to check for any legislation pertaining to the keeping of live specimens.

7.13 Pellet counts

Wood (1988) describes a technique whereby the density of rabbit pellets can be used to estimate population density (Emlen *et al.*, 1957 do so for small mammals). The technique has also been used with deer (Bennett *et al.*, 1940). The problems associated with this technique are reviewed by Neff (1968). It only really works if you can distinguish the pellets of one species from another and if the pellets are deposited in obvious places. With small mammals its use in forests is questionable, but it may be useful for some of the larger non-lagomorph inhabitants of grasslands. Captive specimens may be of help in providing ways of distinguishing pellets in the field (see section 7.12).

7.14 Burrows

Liro (1974) used burrow rewal as an indicator of vole numbers. Otherwise, burrow studies have concentrated on simple descriptions of burrows (e.g. Goyal & Ghosh, 1993; Soriguer & Amat, 1980), or its relation to social organisation (e.g. Mankin & Getz, 1994), or food storage (e.g. Ellison, 1993). The main disadvantages of such studies are that the required excavation needs time, effort and skill and is rather disruptive of the local scenery. You may be able to locate burrows by using soil resistivity measurements (Butler *et al.*, 1994). Airoldi & De Werra (1993) have made theoretical predictions based on computer simulations of water vole burros in different habitats.

If the owner is not excavated or seen it may be identified from the hairs around the burrow (e.g. Sagara *et al.*, 1993) or by using fur pipes (see Section 7.5). Diameter and form may also be species specific (e.g. Sagara *et al.*, 1993).

Burrows often have a unique fauna associated with them (e.g. Anduaga & Halffter, 1991; Deloya, 1991; Gordon & Howden, 1973), the ecology of which may be well worth investigating. See Anduaga & Halffter (1991) for an outline of methodologies.

7.15 Calls

Though many rodents and insectivores vocalise (Dempster & Perrin, 1994; Emmons, 1981), few do so loudly or regularly enough for the calls to be used in censusing. However, calls play an important part in the mating behaviour of some squirrels (Lair, 1990; Smith, 1978; Tamura, 1993; Tamura & Young, 1993), in the territorial behaviour of some marsupials (see Goldingay, 1994 and references therein), lagomorphs (Conner, 1984), and rodents (Hoodless & Morris 1993; Olmos *et al.,* 1993). In these species calls are frequent enough for them to be used to identify species, locate them and give density estimates (though the latter may depend on the season). Hoodless & Morris (1993) and Goldingay (1994) discuss the pros and cons of this type of survey technique.

7.16 Strip census'

This technique, originally developed for surveying birds (Emlen, 1971) and modified for primates (see Eberhardt, 1978; Whitesides *et al.,* 1988) has been also used for sampling some of the larger small mammals (see Cant, 1977; Laurance, 1990; Walker & Cant, 1977) or for seldom seen species a reliable indicator of their presence (e.g. nest for elephant shrews Fitzgibbon & Rathbun 1994).

Simple methods are described in Cant (1977) and the problems raised by changes in detectability between habitats and differences in viewability of different species, along with equations for calculating densities and estimating how many of the sample you may have missed are given by Burnham *et al.,* (1980) and Robinette *et al.,* (1974). These authors also discuss the finer points of methodology.

Strip census cannot be applied with any certainty to small mammals in forest habitats, though it could be adapted for more open ones.

7.17 Miscellanea

There are great many techniques that are species specific, whose utility and applicability rests on some quirk of the biology of the species concerned. A few are given below in the hope of giving ideas for parallel developments.

7.17.1 Scent stations

First used by Linhait & Knowlton (1975), this technique has been widely used to estimate the abundance of fur-bearing mammals, and has also been applied to rabbits, skunks and opossums (Smith *et al.,* 1994). It involves live-capture and individual marking by toe-clipping and the use of an attractant. Visitors are recognised by the patterns they leave in the sand tray surrounding the lure (see Smith *et al.,* 1994 for further information). This is very similar to some of the techniques outlined in Section 6.6.

7.17.2 Arboreal den counts

If species are known to favour particular trees, types or ages of trees or particular habitats, these can be searched for dens. Obviously the accuracy of the assessment will also depend on the ability to detect if the den is in use (possibly using fur pipes, see Section 7.5), or the number of animals that use each den. Den characteristics (e.g. size, smell, gnaw-marks etc.), should also be applied to confirm the identification. Lindenmayer *et al.,* (1991) used this approach, combined with the stagwatching technique (see below) to survey arboreal and scansorial marsupials.

7.17.3 Stagwatching

This technique is useful for studying species that den or nest in trees. It is primarily used for enumeration and censusing. It involves single observers being stationed at previously selected potentially active nest sites, and counting the animals as they move in or out of the den at dusk. This only works if you have a large number of observers who can simultaneously count all the possible trees in a single area and if the animal in question can be identified by it's dusk time silhouette (Lindenmayer *et al.,* 1991; Seebeck *et al.,* 1983; Smith *et al.,* 1989).

7.17.4 Assessment by associated species

Some fungi appear to be specifically associated with the active dens of some mammals species (e.g. Sagara *et al.,* 1993; Taylor, 1994), where they often feed on the mammals dung. If the association is known the presence of the fungus will indicate a burrow which was (at least) recently occupied. The limit to this technique is that, while this type of association is probably quite common, it is rarely recorded. In the limited time available to most expeditions you probably won't be able to conclusively find out as the process of proof in such cases seems to take many years (see Sagara *et al.,* 1993).

7.17.5 Food caches

Some species cache food in good times as an insurance against bad ones (Morris, 1962). This may be stored in a burrow (e.g. Ellison, 1993; Reichman *et al.,* 1985) or buried else where (e.g. Murie, 1977). Investigation of such food stores not only gives an indication of the food eaten by such species but, if it is stored outside a burrow, can give a relative indication of the density of the species concerned (see Smythe, 1978 for further details).

Section Eight
DESCRIBING THE HABITAT

8.1 Qualitative habitat description

Though there are discrepancies on the categorisation of habitat types (e.g. tropical forest; Brown & Lugo, 1990; Corlett, 1994). A brief habitat description should always accompany specimens. This should encompass the general area, the dominant vegetation and any features of special interest (e.g. 'stony bank in *Ocotea*-dominated moist montane forest'). Such descriptions should be made in the field either at the time of each capture or when the traps were set (depending on whether such a comparison is going to form part of your data set). See Nagorsen & Peterson (1980) for information on descriptive techniques.

When an area is trapped, the vegetation should be described in general terms (see Woodall, 1989 as example). This should include the dominant species (or associations) - where practical, in all strata (e.g. ground, shrub, understory and canopy). Estimates of percentage cover of these can also be very useful. Try to note trees or bushes in flower or fruit (if the animals you catch aren't eating them, then why not?). Pay attention to any ecotones and note those traps which are in obviously different habitats. Do not forget to include any features away from the grid that may influence the species you could get or their trappability (e.g. path, road, river, human habitation or agriculture). The habitat choices that separate species living sympatrically can be quite subtle ones (see Kotler *et al.*, 1993; Rogovin, 1992 for examples).

If forest fragments are being trapped, record not only their size (Adler, 1994), but also their shape (Harper *et al.*, 1993) and the number, size and shape of any vegetational classes within them, including altitudinal zonations (Bond *et al.*, 1980). Successional stages may also be important (e.g. Clark, 1994) and should be distinguished as far as possible.

It may be useful to record the distance to other areas of similar habitat type and the presence of otherwise of sources of dispersing animals or barriers to their dispersal. You can get an understanding of the way target animals view the world by simultaneously examining differing scales of habitat utilisation (see de Villiers, 1994).

8.2 Habitat quantification

The quantification of habitat variables provides a way of statistically teasing out those factors which are of importance to the animal in its choice of place.

To do this successfully it is best to have very clear ideas about what you are testing for. Remember that every variable you add means more time in the field and also more time on the computer later. Think how the variables might be associated and try to strip down the number you take to the barest minimum. Try to avoid those that might operate at different levels of cause and effect.

Examples of studies where quantitative techniques have been used include Price (1978, 1982 - microhabitats of desert rodents), Rogovin *et al.,* (1994 - influence of soil type on distribution of desert rodents) van Horne (1982 - quantitative study of groundcover), August (1983 - habitat complexity in a tropical grassland), Fa *et al.,* (1990 - influence of habitat characteristics in a high-altitude grassland), Hayes & Cross (1987) and Tallmon & Mills (1994 - importance of logs to forest rodents) and Woodall (1993 - riverside vegetation and habitat preference in aquatic small mammals). Techniques for the quantification of vertical stratification of vegetation are found in Bond *et al.,* (1980) and Rotenberry & Wiens (1980). Braithwaite (1989) used a semi-quantified technique to assess refuge selection by released small mammals. Note that some patterns of variation in vegetation can be very small scale (see Stowe & Wade, 1979) this analysis may be more precise than you need.

Possibly one of the most complete forms of analysis is given by Dueser & Shugart (1978) who used over twenty variables in their analysis. This seminal paper developed techniques that have been widely copied and modified (see James & Lockerd, 1986). However, be warned, such techniques can take a great deal of time and effort, especially in tropical rainforests. In Amazonian rainforest it took AB and a Brazilian colleague an average of eighty minutes to collect twenty Dueser and Shugart-type data points from each successful trap. This is a heavy investment in time when there are also traps to check, bait and lay and specimens to process.

8.3 Microclimates

Microclimatic studies are quite detailed and probably involve more equipment and effort than most expeditions would wish to devote to the topic. Nevertheless, they can reveal the subtleties of a species interaction with its environment (e.g. Du Plessis *et al.,* 1992; Read, 1989). Such studies generally involve investigation of the temperature and humidity ranges of the burrow and nest systems or refuges of the target species (e.g. Dawson & Denny, 1969; Gettinger, 1975; Du Plessis & Kerley, 1991). Studies of the physical tolerances of the animals themselves are unethical.

Section Nine
RECORDING DATA

9.1 Data sheets and note books

The written data set is vital. Without it your work is wasted and whatever material you have collected is pretty close to useless. Duplicating your records is dealt with in Section 9.3.

Your records should be clear, concise and capable of being used easily by someone else. Avoid codes and abbreviations whenever possible. If you must use them then make sure that you have an accompanying explanatory glossary - it is amazing how easily you forget your own notations. Preparing xeroxed field data sheets in advance is helpful as they help maintain clarity and act as a checklist of things to do and data to take. If you must change what information is included part way through the fieldwork, make sure that an explanation is clearly given in your field notebook. Delany (1974) gives good examples of data sheet layout.

Loose sheets are useful while dissecting but, unless they are bound in a ringbinder (not forgetting the reinforcers), such notes should be copied into a proper hardcovered notebook. It is not normally necessary to go to the extreme of getting a waterproof notebooks but can be useful (see Sections 13.1.6 and 13.2.6), but do take care to keep such documents out of the wet. Check for termite damage too.

Remember to write in pencil as ink and biro tend to run, it is difficult to write with them on wet paper, and pencil is much more resistant if solvent (alcohol) is spilt on it. When using a notebook (as opposed to using data sheets) to record data, prepare a guideline form and stick this to the cover of your notebook so you don't forget what to write down. This has the advantage over data sheets of not blowing around in the wind and being easier to stuff into a pocket. Aquascribe waterproof notebooks have a clear plastic pocket ideal for inserting such a guideline form.

9.2 Keeping the collection safe

The specimens should be kept away from mould and insects. Drying of skins can be aided by wrapping them in absorbent paper (newspaper will do), putting them in a plant press, changing the paper regularly and checking for insects and fungal infection. Putting silica gel inside sealed bags will ensure an adequate level of protective dessication (use the variety that changes colour if saturated).

Once dried, the collection may be kept in such presses or crated up. There is no need to invest in expensive boxes - but placing the specimens in sawdust or similar in a well-aired box is an essential precaution. A small amount of insecticide can be added (e.g. mothballs), but try not to get this in contact with the skins as it can discolour them.

As a matter of general policy never put all your specimens in the same box, nor all boxes in the same place. Split the collection up. This guards against accidents (fire, theft etc).

NOTE: Many insecticides, formerly in common use, are now considered to be carcinogenic. Others can cause bad discolouration of any collected skins. Check with museum staff before embarking.

9.3 Keeping the data safe

The same paranoia should be applied to the written data. Try always to keep duplicate field notebooks. When travelling don't put both in the same rucksack. Make photocopies of your data and deposit one set at a safe place in town whenever you have the opportunity. Sending home a set of the data is another option. Such pains are worthwhile - if you lose your notes you are very unlikely to be able to remember all that you did or the precise situation under which specimens were obtained and you will have wasted all of your field time and effort. Be paranoid, the Royal Geographical Society has heard of expeditions where this has actually happened.

9.4 Labelling - the do's and the don'ts

Never leave labelling till later. It might be a bit tedious but it is the lifeline that connects your specimens to the written data. The best labels are those of stiff paper or card to which thin string or cotton is attached via a brass ring. These are normally available from a museum of university department. Labels such as this can be marked either in 2B pencil or in Indian ink (using a Rotaring or similar). Write clearly and concisely. Avoid abbreviations. You should write considering that your label may be read in a century's time by someone who's first language is not English. Your label may well be all they have to go on.

All labels should have: your collection number (all pieces and parts of the same animal have the same collection number), date (day, month as a letter abbreviation and the year in full), the name of the expedition, name of collector, country, locality, grid reference, altitude, habitat type, species (leave blank if unsure), sex, reproductive condition. When the specimens are being accessioned, a museum will add its own collection number to all this.

Many museums and departments have specially printed labels with these categories on. These are very helpful as they save you time, aid legibility and act as a check list. It is sensible to have worked out your labelling regime in advance as part of your pre-fieldwork preparation.

Labels should be attached firmly and safely. Don't tie them too tightly as then they can damage the specimen when people move them to look at the information. Leave as much of the string free as possible. Tie the label on so that it is difficult for it to slip off (in choosing the place of attachment remember that even in the best run collection specimens do get buffeted and broken). The hind foot is standard for skins, the zygomatic arch for skulls. Bottles are generally labelled by placing one label inside (facing outwards) and tying another to the specimen. Always use officially-supplied labels for labelling wet-preserved materials, anything else has an irritating tendency to fall apart very quickly and then be of absolutely no use whatsoever.

Section Ten
SPECIMEN IDENTIFICATION

10.1 General considerations

Because of pressures on museum staff, you may well have to do your own identifications. It is therefore advisable to become as familiar as possible with your material and the associated literature. Try to get all original papers relating to the description of the species that could (on geographic grounds) possibly occur in your area (make the region of reference fairly broad as range extensions are not uncommon finds from expedition work). There will probably be quite a lot of technical terms that are unfamiliar to you - do not guess or skip them - ask the staff of the museum or institution.

Familiarity with the literature and specimens is something you should have before you go. It aids fieldwork and cuts down on the amount of post-expedition work. Many of the common groups of small mammals (e.g. *Akodon*, *Proechimys* and *Marmosa* in Neotropics; *Mastomys* and *Praomys* in Africa; *Rattus* in Asia) are in a state of taxonomic confusion and have been for many years. Name changes are frequent. To avoid confusion and to ensure that you and your references agree about the nomenclature it is best to check the taxonomic literature for any recent reclassifications. The universal standard is now Wilson & Reeder (1993), which has replaced Honacki *et al.,* (1982). Most journals accept the classifications they proposed, and it is very useful for sorting out the potential confusions over synonyms, especially when referring to some of the older literature.

Whenever possible, try to do the bulk of identifications in institutions in the host country. This forges academic links with the scientists there and may have a number of other practical benefits (see Section 11.1). Many such institutions are under-resourced, so try to take crucial papers with you and leave copies.

To aid fieldwork and reduce impact of collecting, try to construct a key that permits field identification and does not require killing (e.g. Lidicker & Laurance, 1990). Such keys should concentrate on visual characteristics e.g. pelage colour and pattern and use measurements only where necessary. This reduces handling time and minimises the chances of animals dying of fright. Remember when constructing the key that colours and dimensions of animals may have been changed a bit by preservation (Bininda-Emonds & Russel, 1994), and it may be necessary to refer to the species original description (which you will find referenced in Wilson & Reeder, 1993). Objective assessment of colours may be difficult (see Zuk & Decruyenaere, 1994).

Though several colour standards exist, they are generally expensive and not all that easily carried (and colour photocopiers are not accurate enough to be of use). You may find it easier to use a paint chart and refer back to the manufacturer for the official designation of the colour used. It may be useful to take a photo file compiled from museum specimens in the UK.

10.2 New species

There is always the chance you will find something new (see for example, Rickart & Heaney, 1991). The rules of nomenclature are quite complex and the procedures associated with the announcement of a new species rather precise. It is, however, unwise to rush into print. Be cautious. Consult widely. Ask the advice of museum staff over precise procedure.

Section Eleven
POST-FIELDWORK ACTIVITIES

11.1 Dispersion of specimens

It is most inadvisable to try to take home the whole of your expedition's collection. Such action is likely to lead to accusations of neo-colonialism and make difficult any planned future field work (by you or others). Identification of specimens at host country institutions (see Section 10.1) should alleviate the need to take great numbers of specimens away. Most institutions are amenable to a split on a "one-for-you one-for-us" basis. The only likely sticking point are 'unicates', those you have just one of. Inevitably these will be the most interesting things in the collection. If you have built up a good working relationship with the institutions of the host country it should be possible to work out a basis for a loan, to be returned once the material has been identified. It is unwise to try and do things in a clandestine way since, if the specimen yield interesting results, such underhandedness it may prove embarrassing when trying to publish results.

Do not give the host country all the dross and save the best specimens for yourself (for one thing, they might take such specimens to be the apogee of your ability). Ensure that complete copies of all field notes accompany such specimens and that copies of any additional notes are also presented.

11.2 Customs, CITES and documentation

An export licence is almost always required for scientific collections. You should check the precise nature and form before you go. Many countries require that you have liaised with a designated authority (e.g. the national museum), and require written proof of this before they will issue an export licence for specimens. In addition to customs control small mammals (especially rodents) are often the business of the Ministry of Public Health and/or the Ministry of Agriculture. You may also have to get permits from them before the material is allowed out of the country. Allow time for this between finishing fieldwork and leaving the country (usually double the amount of time you first thought of).

In order that you have academic credibility it is useful to have a letter saying that the specimens that you are taking away will be deposited in some internationally recognised repository (a national museum in UK or one at a University), and will not be going into your own private collection. Such a letter should have been formulated in advance and bought out with you, with the references to the material to be deposited couched in general terms.

If you try and smuggle out your material you risk getting it impounded at the out-going airport. This will cause much of the value of your fieldwork to be lost; it will lose you credibility and upset things for people in the future; and it will be difficult to publish on the material. Arrival at the UK end can also be a problem - with no papers your material is equally likely to be impounded at this end.

CITES stands for Convention on International Trade in Endangered Species of Wild Fauna and Flora. It is an international convention whereby rare, endangered and threatened species of animal and plant are placed on categories (appendices) that indicate how restricted is the movement of specimens of that species (I - no international trade allowed, through to III where it is permitted in certain circumstances). Though your collection may not have any rare species in it the host country may wish to put it through CITES documentation. Do not object as UK Customs (hardly surprisingly) can be very suspicious about collections coming in from overseas. A CITES certificate may stop them impounding your material.

Information about CITES and UK requirements can be obtained from the Department of the Environment in Bristol (See Section 13.2.9). This office can also deal with general enquiries about import restrictions into the UK. The laws change from time to time and so it is best to check before you go to make sure that you do all you can to meet the current regulations.

11.3 Writing up

It cannot be stressed strongly enough the importance that your work is written up, published and distributed. If you don't do that then it wasn't an expedition, but an exotic holiday that you conned other people into paying for.

11.3.1 Reports

It is important to get a preliminary report out quickly. This will help you organise the data and see what else must be done before publication. If possible, a short report should be prepared (in the language of the host country, if possible, or with at least a summary in that language) before you leave.

Do not stop at the preliminary report stage. Do a full report. Distribute it widely (in doing so remember how frustrated you became when trying to track down obscure expedition reports). Distribute your final report widely, send copies to all the copyright libraries and any 'specialists' who may have an interest in your results. Don't forget the British Museum Natural History and Zoological Society (London) libraries. For a full list of potential recipients see Barnett (1994). Winser (1992) provides guidelines for report writing and format.

Include at least a summary of your work in the language of the host country and ensure that this is sent back as soon as possible to the relevant institutions within it. It may be a good idea to produce a short report (a page or two in the local language) before you leave the country, apart from political benefits this is helpful for pulling data together and focusing everyone's minds.

11.3.2 Papers

Do publish your results in a proper journal (a popular account is not really sufficient). Guidance on how to publish a scientific paper is given by Barnett (1994). Even a short note is better than nothing. Don't feel that your work is unworthy. Even snippets are valuable. Nothing will have been achieved if the results of all the hard work simply sit in a file on a shelf and gather dust. In addition to a (perhaps small) contribution to a well-known and widely circulated journal, try and publish also in journals of the host country in the host country's language (many of the national museums have a bulletin which will serve this purpose). Though not all are as widely read, such journals are an important medium for spreading the data you obtained and for advancing the internationalisation of science. International journals can be very expensive, so try to ensure that copies or reprints of your contribution are sent back to the appropriate institutions in the host country.

While the choice of local journal is obviously expedition specific, this short list may help in choosing a journal to submit a paper for wider readership: *Acta Theriologica, African Journal of Ecology, Animal Ecology, Australian Mammalogy, Biodiversity and Conservation, Biotropica, Ecology*, *Journal of Mammalogy*, *Journal of Tropical Ecology, Journal of Zoology, Lutra, Mammalia, Oryx, South African Journal of Zoology, , Studies in Neotropical Fauna and Environment, Tropical Biology, Zeitschrift fur Saugeitkunde* (*society membership prerequisite). Wherever possible you should aim to produce a paper in the language of the host country in a journal published in the host country.

Any published paper should always have a summary in the language of the host country (whether it is a requirement of the journal or not). Always send copies of your papers and reports back to institutions and individuals in the host country. Always acknowledge help where it was given (or, if politics dictate, where it was supposed to have been). Always send reprints back to the host country.

Finally, do not be put off from publishing. So little is known about small mammals in general that even a short natural history-type note is often of immense value (see Barnett, 1991 as an example of a simple paper of this type).

Section Twelve
DATA ANALYSIS

12.1 What to look for
The data set you have can be divided up into two parts; the specimens themselves and the trapping data. Both can be a fertile source of information. It would be sensible to examine the likely type of data analysis applicable to your studies before departing into the field. Data sets from the specimens could include:

- size differences between species, populations, sexes
- presence of size classes within catch
- reproduction periodicity
- dental abnormalities

Data sets from the information collected while trapping could include:
- habitat preferences (by species, sex or age-class)
- differences in trapping success over time within same site
- clustering of trap successes (due to resource clumping?)
- differences between sites
- differences in trap success between different makes or types of trap
- differences due to different methodologies (types of bait, setting operation, trap check times)
- if previous occupant makes a difference (sex, species)
- density estimations
- estimations of species diversity

There are a number of caveats to the interpretation of the data. Essentially these revolve around the limitations of trapping as a technique. They include:
- differential trappability of age classes, sexes and species.
- differential trappability of habitat types
- inter-worker variability

The first has been a great preoccupation amongst field workers, especially the differences between sexes and age classes. This stems from the time when small mammal ecology concentrated very much on the study of the mechanisms governing population regulation. Useful references include

Buskirk & Lindstedt (1989), Zhu (1985) for sex biases; and Mihok (1984) for bias between age-cohorts. For an explanation of why these exist see Korn (1986) (also Clark, 1980; van Horne, 1982).

While a lot of work has been devoted to the first point very little has been devoted to the latter two (though there are some botanical examples, see Hall & Okali, 1978). They are obviously very difficult to quantify, and, equally obviously, could make a huge difference to how many animals were caught and hence the apparent diversity or density of the small mammal fauna. Attempts to quantify these could make a useful study in themselves (though not one that would require an expedition).

In addition, it is possible to infer something about the organisation of the small communities from the relative sizes of their constituent species (see Gatz, 1981 for an example of this approach). The study of body sizes and of skull dimensions are considered key characters for such types of analysis (see Hespenheide, 1973; Oksanen et al., 1979). Given that they represent the sum of all the interacting competitive forces in the year, their analysis may give a better understanding of the forces structuring the community than is otherwise possible with data gathered on a short field trip (see Feinsinger et al., 1981; Hespenheide, 1973; Holdbrook, 1982).

12.2 Statistics for various methodologies

There are almost as many statistical tests for analysing the data as there are traps to get the animals with or, indeed, types of animals to obtain. All tests make assumptions and it is a matter of experience which ones apply or do not apply to the work you have done. Even the apparently simple estimation of trap success can be fraught with difficulties (see Simonetti, 1986). Many of the statistical tests are simply not designed to cope with freak incidences like two mice in one snap-trap (see Kaufman & Kaufman, 1988). The estimation of abundance from trapping data can also be problematic and is very much dependent on the statistical technique used (Doncaster & Micol, 1988 provide a salutary example). Other useful papers include Horacek (1984), Montgomery (1987) and Tepper (1967) for statistics relating to capture-mark-recapture studies; Jett & Nichols (1987) and Nichols (1986) for density estimates; Goodman (1984) has reviewed the statistics of reproductive rate estimates and Boutin & Krebs (1986) provide useful data on the estimation of survival rates. Matson (1982) provides a useful introduction to techniques of biogeographical analysis of species distributions.

A good general overview of statistical techniques for small mammals is provided by Delany (1974) and Flowerdew (1976), while Krebs (1989) is a key resource which brings together a diverse array of statistical methodologies. Other interesting papers include Hayne (1949), Skalski & Robson (1992) and Southern (1973).

NOTE: as mentioned in Section 11.3, your work is quite likely to be worthy of publication even if it is of a basic nature. Do not be put off if you do not have the kind of data that can be analysed statistically.

Section Thirteen
EQUIPMENT AND MANUFACTURERS

13.1 Equipment

What equipment you take will depend on the aims of the expedition. For those who like to be frugal, it is worth remembering that its better to be over rather than under equipped. You won't be able to go back and get the bits you didn't take.

In many countries you may be able to purchase items such as cord for festooning and material for drift nets. One expedition is known to have had their live traps made locally, based on the Sherman design (though care should be taken here - you don't want to be responsible for the wholesale decimation of small mammal populations by passing on 'western' technology). However, in some countries even basic supplies are hard to come by, therefore be sure, or take everything with you.

13.1.1 Traps

The choice of trap has already been discussed earlier in this book (Sections 2.1.1 and 2.2). It is best to be prepared to carry out field maintenance, both Longworth and Sherman produce a variety of spare parts and it may be worth taking an assortment. However if space and budget is limited nothing replaces ingenuity and a bit of araldite!

13.1.2 Spring balances

A set of spring balances are vital for any small mammal fieldwork. A graded series of balances from 0-100g, 0-500g and 0-1000g are normally sufficient. The two main makes are Pesola and Salter and it is a matter of personal preference as to which is best. The Pesolas are Swiss made in metal with an accuracy of +/-0.3%, the Salters are made in plastic and maintain their accuracy well. Those people who are used to Pesolas do not find using Salters so easy to use, however the converse is also true! Possibly the deciding factor will be cost, the Salters cast approximately a third of the Pesolas.

13.1.3 Callipers

These are used for taking body measurements and a good pair are invaluable. Two types are available, with or without a dial, and can be made of metal or plastic. Callipers with a dial are easier to read to an accuracy of 0.1mm, though measurements to the nearest 1mm are normal. We favour those made by Camlab which are made from reinforced polyamide, lightweight and easy to use.

13.1.4 Biological supplies

Taking sufficient scalpels, forceps, latex gloves etc to do the job is vital. It would probably be best to purchase these from a college/university's biological store if possible as they tend to get bulk discount from suppliers. If this is not possible see the list of suppliers in Section 13.2.4.

13.1.5 Headtorches

Headtorches are invaluable for any expedition undertaking nocturnal studies. They are also useful for expeditions in general allowing both hands free for things like visiting the little expeditioners' room! Petzl probably make the best ones on the market, with three models currently available. The Micro, though compact and lightweight is probably too whimpy for expedition use, leaving a choice between the Zoom and Mega.

Both have rotating front bezels which, in addition to turning the lamp on and off, focuses the beam from flood to spot. They are proofed against rain (though not totally waterproof), the lamp unit pivots vertically and the rear battery box counterbalances the lamp. The zoom runs off a 4.5v flat battery which, with the standard bulb, offers a life of 17 hours. The standard FR21 bulb only has a 30m range, by fitting a FR22 halogen this can be increased to 100m though reducing the battery life to between a third and a half. The normal flat battery is difficult to obtain in many countries and therefore an adapter which allows the use of 3xAA batteries is a useful addition.

The Mega comes with a halogen bulb as standard and uses three C size batteries. This gives a range of 100m and a battery life of 11 hours. In emergencies 3xAA batteries can be used, though reducing battery life to 2 hours 45 minutes. The choice is personal but the Megan is heavier and bulkier, We prefer a Zoom with halogen bulb. These can be purchased from most outdoor shops, if not try Field & Trek (see Section 13.2.5).

13.1.6 Notebooks

Some expeditioners think that waterproof notebooks are overkill, though from experience they can be very useful. Two makes are available, Aquascribe and Chartwell, Aquascribe having the greatest range. In addition, if you are really organised and prepare you survey sheets in advance it is even possible to get both A4 and A3 waterproof photocopy paper, though at some cost.

Whatever type of notebook or paper used, either waterproof or normal, remember that it is preferable to write in pencil as ink (including biro) tends to run when wet.

13.1.7 Tying and tagging

Getting hold of nylon cord for "festooning" and trap tying should not prove a problem. Reels containing 200m can be obtained from ships chandlers (among others) though it may be advisable to give advanced warning otherwise they are unlikely to have sufficient.

JSP Limited make several types of high visibility tape suitable for making into tags. Glo-tape (25mm wide) comes in 27.5m rolls and is a plastic-like tape. It is difficult to tie (the knots slip) and fades with time. Fabglo and Nylotape (both 20mm wide) come in 20m rolls and are easier to tie. All three can be written on using suitable pens (waterproof OHP markers work).

13.1.8 Trapping box

It may be useful to have all equipment needed for processing catches in a trapping box. This keeps everything together and means nothing will be forgotten when leaving base! There are numerous tool boxes on the market which can be adapted to individual needs with a bit of ingenuity and DIY.

13.1.9 Tracking equipment

Radio and transponder tracking equipment is somewhat expensive. It is therefore advisable to take advice on the type of equipment suitable for the project in question. If you have a choice use waterproof receivers even in dry environments as they are more dust proof and you never know when accidents might happen! Remember that some countries may be a little jumpy about unfamiliar electronic gizmos so be sure to check and if necessary get clearance (and keep the letters giving you this clearance in a prominent accessible place; keep extra copies too).

Computer programmes are available for radio tracking data analysis. The two most common in the UK are Ranges IV (for PCs) and Wildtrack (for Apple Macs), the latter being the most user friendly.

13.1.10 Safari/fishing vests

These are incredibly practical for small mammal work and not too heavy to wear in hot climates. If you don't want to use a trapping box their numerous pockets can be utilised to hold all bits and bobs needed for specimen processing. It is best not to look like a badly disguised CIA agent, therefore shy away from colours associated with military/paramilitary organisations.

13.1.11 Miscellanea

Altimeters are useful if examining the altitudinal range of species and are available from Field & Trek. Beta lights, used for following larger species at night (see Section 7.8) can be purchased from Biotrak or Saunders-Roe. Brass eyelet's for drift nets (see Section 2.6.2) are available in a variety of sizes from Pointnorth Ltd.

13.2 Manufacturers

Some manufacturers are willing to support expeditions, though the days of totally free equipment are probably over. When making overtures to this end remember you will not be the first, or last, expedition to do so. Consequently always, always remember to personally thank those who have helped you in any way whatsoever.

13.2.1 Traps

Penlon Ltd   (Longworth & Field Trip Traps)
Radley Road
Abingdon   Tel: 01235 554222
Oxon OX14 3PH   Fax: 01235 555252

H.B. Sherman Inc   (Sherman Traps)
P.O. Box 20267
Tallahassee
Florida 32316   Tel: (904) 562 5566
USA   Fax: (904) 562 4234

Havahart Ltd   (Havahart Traps)
Box 551
Ossining
New York
USA

Thomas's Europe   (Small Trip Trap)
Oakwell Way
Birstall
Bately   Tel: (01924) 474373
West Yorkshire WF17 9LU   Fax: (01924) 470961

Rentokil Ltd   (Trap-Ease Mouse Trap)
Felcourt
East Grinstead
West Sussex RH19 2JY   Tel: (01342) 833022

Selfset Ltd   (Metal Snap Traps)
Falcon Works
Hanworth Road   Tel: (01932) 784225
Sunbury-on-Thames TW16 5DE   Fax: (01932) 788175

Procter Bros Ltd   (Nipper Snap Traps)
Pantglas Ind Estate
Bedwas
Newport   Tel: (01222) 882111
Gwent NP1 8XD   Fax: (01222) 887005

13.2.2 Spring balances
British Trust for Ornithology (Pesola & Salter)
The Nunnery,
Nunnery Place
Thetford   Tel: (01842) 750050
Norfolk IP24 2PU   Fax: (01842) 750030

Salter Abbey Weighing Machines Ltd (Salter)
St Botolph's Lane
Bury St Edmonds   Tel: (01284) 61321
Suffolk IP33 2AX   Fax: (01284) 750335

13.2.3 Callipers
Camlab Limited   (Camlab Callipers)
Nuffield Road   Tel: (01223) 424222
Cambridge CB4 1TH   Fax: (01223) 420856

13.2.4 Biological supplies
BDH Laboratory Supplies
Merck Ltd
Hunter Boulevard
Lutterworth   Tel: 0800 223344
Leicestershire LE17 4XN   Fax: (01455) 558586

Fisons Scientific Equipment
Bishop Meadow Road
Loughborough   Tel: (01509) 231166
Leicestershire LE11 0RG   Fax: (01509) 231893

13.2.5 Headtorches
Field & Trek   (Outdoor Equipment)
3 Wates Way
Brentwood   Tel: (01277) 233122
Essex CM15 9TB   Fax: (01277) 260789

13.2.6 Notebooks
Hawkins & Manwaring   (Aquascribe)
Westborough
Newark   Tel: (01400) 81492
Notts NG23 5HJ   Fax: (01400) 81375

H.W. Peel & Company Ltd   (Chartwell)
Chartwell House
Lyon Way
Greenford   Tel: (0181) 578 6861
Middlesex UB6 0BN   Fax: (0181) 575 8253

13.2.7 Trap tagging
JSP Ltd   (Glo, Fabglo & Nylo Tapes)
Worsham Mill
Minster Lovell
Oxford OX8 5RX   Tel: (01993) 824000

13.2.8 Tracking and marking
Biotrack Ltd   (Radio Tracking Equipment)
52 Furzebrook Road
Wareham   Tel: (01929) 552992
Dorset BH20 5AX   Fax: (01929) 554948

Mariner Radar Ltd   (Radio Tracking Equipment)
Bridleway
Campsheath
Lowestoft   Tel: (01502) 567195
Suffolk NR32 5DN   Fax: (01502) 508762

Institute of Terrestrial Ecology (Ranges IV)
Furzebrook Research Station
Furzebrook Road
Wareham   Tel: (01929) 551518/9
Dorset BH20 5AS   Fax: (01929) 551087

ISIS Innovation Ltd   (Wildtrack)
Dept. Zoology
University of Oxford
South Parks Road
Oxford OX1 3PS

RS Biotech   (Transponders for Marking and Tracking)
Brook Street
Alva
Clackmannanshire   Tel: (01259) 760335
FK12 6JJ   Fax: (01259) 762824

Animalcare Ltd   (Transponders for Marking)
Common Road
Dunnington   Tel: (01904) 488661
York YO1 5RU   Fax: (01904) 488184

Radiant Color Inc   (Pigment for Powder Tracking)
2800 Radiant Road
Richmond
CA 94804USA

13.2.9 Miscellanea
Field & Trek   (Altimeters)
As Section 13.2.5 above.

Biotrack   (Betalights)
As Section 13.2.8 above.

Saunders-Roe Ltd   (Betalights)
Millington Road
Hayes   Tel: (0181) 573 3800
Middlesex UB3 4AZ   Fax: (0181) 561 3436

Pointnorth Ltd   (Brass Eyelets)
16/18 Newry Fawr
Holyhead
Anglesey
Gwynedd LL65 1LB   Tel: (01407) 760195

Department of the Environment (CITES Info)
Wildlife Trade Licensing Branch
Room 822
Tollgate House
Houlton Street   Tel: (0117) 9878691
Bristol BS2 9DJ   Fax: (0117) 9878206

Merrist Wood College   (Tree Climbing Courses)
Worplesdon
Guildford
Surrey   Tel: (01483) 232424
GU3 3PE   Fax: (01483) 236518

Section Fourteen
REFERENCES

Adamczewska-Andrzejewska, K.A. (1971) Methods of age determination in *Apodemus agrarius* (Pallas 1771). *Annals Zoologica Fennicki* 8: 68-71.

Adamczewska-Andrzejewska, K.A. (1973) Growth variation and age criteria in *Apodemus agrarius* (Pallas 1771). *Acta Theriologica* 18: 353-394.

Adler, G.H. (1994) Tropical forest fragmentation and isolation promote asynchrony among populations of a frugivorous rodent. *Journal of Animal Ecology* 63: 903-911.

Airoldi, J.P. & de Werra, D. (1993) The burrow system of the fossorial form of the water vole (*Arvicola terrestris scherman* Shaw.) (Mammalia, Rodentia): an approach using graph theoretical methods and simulation models. *Mammalia* 57: 423-433.

Aitken, P.F. (1977a) The little pigmy possum (*Cercartetus lepidus* [Thomas]) found living on the Australian mainland. *South Australian Naturalist* 51: 63-66.

Aitken, P.F. (1977b) Re-discovery of the swamp Antechinus in south Australia after 37 years. *South Australian Naturalist* 52: 28-30.

Alibhai, S.K. & Key, G. (1985) A preliminary investigation of small mammal biology in the Kora national reserve, Kenya. *Journal of Tropical Ecology* 1: 321-327.

Aldous, S.E. (1940) A method of marking beavers. *Journal of Wildlife Management* 4: 145-148.

Alho, C.A.H., Pereira, L.A., & Paula A.C. (1986) Patterns of habitat utilization by small mammal populations in the cerrado biome of central Brazil. *Mammalia* 50: 447-460.

Andersen, J. & Jensen, B. (1972) The weight of the eye lens in European hares of known age. *Acta Theriologica* 17: 87-92.

Anderson, S. & Long, C.A. (1961) Small mammals in pellets of barn owls from Minaca, Mexico. *American Museum Novitates* No. 2052: 1-3.

Anderson, B.W. & Ohmart, R.D. (1977) Rodent baite addative which repels insects. *Journal of Mammalogy* 58: 242.

Anderson, T.J.C., Berry, A.J., Amos, J.N., & Cook, J.M. (1988) Spool-and-line tracking of the New Guinea Spiny Bandicoot, *Echymiptera kalubu* (Marsupialia: Paramelidae). *Journal of Mammalogy.* 69: 114-120.

Anduaga, S. Halffter, P. (1991) Escarabajos asociados a modrigueras de roedores (Coleoptera; Scarabaeidae, Scarabaeiinae). *Folia Entomologica Mexicana* 81: 185-197.

Angerbjorn, A. (1986) Reproduction in mountain hares (*Lepus timidus*) in relation to density and physical condition. *Journal of Zoology* (London) 208: 59-568.

Askanar, T. & Hansson, L. (1970) The eye lens as an age indicator in small rodents. *Oikos* 18: 151-153.

Aslin, H.J. (1976) Discovery of a new dasyurid marsupial in south Australia. *South Australian Naturalist* 50: 39-41.

Atkinson, P.W., Dutton, J.S., Peet, N.B. & Sequeira, V.A.S. (1994) *A study of the birds, small mammals, turtles and medicinal plants of São Tomé with notes on Príncipe*. Birdlife International Study Report No. 56, Birdlife International, Cambridge.

Atramentowicz, M. (1986) Dynamique de population chez trois marsupiaux didephides de Guyane. *Biotropica* 18: 136-149.

August, P.V. (1983) The role of habitat complexity and heterogenaity in structuring tropical small mammal communities *Ecology* 64: 1495-1507.

Bailey, G.N.A. (1968) Trap-shyness in a woodland population of bank voles (*Clethrionomys glareous*). *Journal of Zoology* (London) 156: 517-521.

Baker, S.J. & Clarke, C.N. (1988) Cage trapping of coypus (*Myocastor coypus*) on baited rafts. *Journal of Applied Ecology* 25: 41-48.

Baker, G.D. & Degabriele, R. (1987) The diet of the red fox (*Vulpes vulpes*) in the Eldorado hills of north-east Victoria. *Victorian Naturalist* 104: 39-42.

Bammer, G., Barnett, S.A. & Marples, T.G. (1988) Responses to novelty by the Australian swamp rat, *Rattus lutreolus* (Rodentia: Muridae). *Australian Mammalogy* 11: 63-66.

Banta, B. (1957) A simple trap for collecting desert reptiles. *Herpetologica* 13: 174-176.

Barnett, A.P. (1991) Records of the grey-bellied shrew opossum, *Caenolestes caniventer* and Tate's shrew opossum, *Caenolestes tatei* (Caenolestidae, Marsupialia) from Ecuadorian montane forests. *Mammalia* 55: 443-445.

Barnett, A. (1994) *Writing and publishing scientific papers*. Expedition Advisory Centre, London.

Barnett, S.A. (1981) *The Rat: a study in behaviour*. Chicago University Press, Chicago.

Barnett, A.A. & Da Cunha, A.C. (1994) Notes on the small mammals of Ilha de Maracá, Roraima state, Brazil. *Mammalia* 58: 131-137.

Barry, R.E. (1976) Mucosal surface areas and villous morphology of the small intestine of small mammals: functional interpretations. *Journal of Mammalogy* 57: 273-290.

Barry, R.E. (1977) Length and absorptive surface area apportionment of segments of the hindgut for eight species of small mammals. *Journal of Mammalogy* 58: 419:420.

Bateman, J. (1971) *Animal Traps and Trapping*. David & Charles, Newton Abbot.

Batzli, G.O. & Cole, F.R. (1979) Nutritional ecology of microtine rodents: digestability of forage. *Journal of Mammalogy* 60: 740-750.

Baxter, R.M. (1993) Banded mongoose predation on a shrew, *Crocidura f. flavescens*. *Mammalia* 57: 145-146.

Beattie, A. (1971) A technique for the study of insect-borne pollen. *Pan-Pacific Entomologist* 47: 82.

Bekker. J.P. (1986) A time-clock construction, connected with a Longworth trap. *Lutra* 29: 224-227.

Bellamy, R. (1992) *Expedition Field Techniques: Ethnobiology in Tropical Forests*. Expedition Advisory Centre, London.

Beltyukova, O.P. & Spassky, Y.V. (1989) An ant-proof trap for smaller mammals. *Zoologicheskii Zhurnal* 68: 124-125.

Bennett, L.J., English, P.F. & McCain, R. (1940) A study of deer populations by use of pellet-group counts. *Journal of Wildlife Management* 4: 398-403.

Bennett, A.F., Schultz, M., Lumsden, L.F., Robertson, P. & Johnson, P.G. (1989) Pitfall trapping of small mammals in temperate forests of southeastern Australia. *Australian Mammal* 12: 37-39.

Bergstrom, B.J. (1986) An analysis of multiple captures in *Peromyscus* (*Peromyscus*) with a critique on methodology. *Canadian Journal of Zoology*. 64: 1407-1411.

Bergstrom, B.J. & Sauer, J.R. (1986) Social travelling inferred from multiple captures: testing assumptions. *American Midland Naturalist* 115: 201-203.

Bergstrom, B. (1988) Home range of three species of chipmunk (*Tamias*) as assessed by radiotelemetry and grid trapping. *Journal of Mammalogy* 69: 190-193.

Berry, A.J., Anderson, T.J.C. Amos, J.N. & Cook, J.M. (1987) Spool-and-line tracking of giant rats in New Guinea. *Journal of Zoology* (London) 213: 299-303.

Bhadresa, R.(1977) Food preferences of rabbits *Oryctolagus cuniculus* L. at Holkham sand dunes, Norfolk. *Journal of Applied Ecology* 14: 287-291.

Bhadresa, R. (1981) *Indentification of leaf epidermal fragments in rabbit faeces (with reference to heathland vegetation)*. Rogate Field Centre Papers, No. 4. Kings College, London.

Bhadresa, R.(1987) Rabbit grazing studies in a grassland community using faecal analysis and exclosures. *Field Studies* 6: 657-684.

Bider, J.R. (1968) Animal activity in uncontrolled terrestrial communities as determined by a sand transect technique. *Ecological Monographs* 38: 269-308.

Biknevicius, A.R. (1993) Biochemical scaling of limb bones and differential limb use in caviomorph rodents. *Journal of Mammalogy* 74: 95-107.

Bininda-Emonds, O.R.P. & Russell, A.P. (1994) Flight style in bats as predicted from wing morphology: the effects of specimen preservation. *Journal of Zoology* (London) 234: 275-287.

Blotekjaer, K., Langvatn, R., Pettersen, P.O. & Oygarden, J. (1978) An electronic device for automatic counting of red deer *Cervus elephus* moving along tracks. *Oikos* 30: 448-451.

Bond, W., Ferguson, M. & Forsyth, G. (1980) Small mammals and habitat structure along altitudinal gradients in the southern Cape mountains. *South African Journal of Zoology* 15: 34-43.

Boutin, S. & Krebs, C.J. (1986) Estimating survival rates of snowshoe hares. *Journal of Wildlife Management* 50: 592-594.

Boonstra, R., Kanter, M. & Krebs, C.J. (1992) A tracking technique to locate small mammals at low densities. *Journal of Mammalogy* 73: 683-685.

Boonstra, R. & Krebs, C.J. (1978) Pitfall trapping of *Microtus townsendii*. *Journal of Mammalogy* 59: 136-148.

Boonstra, R., Gilbert, B.S. & Krebs, C.J. (1993) Mating systems and sexual dimorphism in mass in microtines. *Journal of Mammalogy* 74: 224-229.

Boonstra, R. & Rodd, F.H. (1982) Another potential bias in the use of the Longworth trap. *Journal of Mammalogy* 63: 672-675.

Booth, E.S. (1944) Temporary preservation of small mammals in the field. *Journal of Mammalogy* 25: 354-358.

Borell, A.E. (1938) Cleaning small collections of skulls with dermestid beetles. *Journal of Mammalogy* 19: 102-103.

Le Boulenge-Nguyen, P.Y. & Le Boulenge, E. (1986) A new ear-tag for small mammals. *Journal of Zoology* (London) 209: 302-304.

Le Boulenge, E. & Le Boulenge-Nguyen, P.Y. (1987) A cost-effective live trap for small mammals. *Acta Theriologica* 32: 140-144.

Boutin, S. & Krebs, C.J. (1986) Estimating survival rates for snowshoe hares. *Journal of Wildlife Management* 50: 592-594.

Bowen, W.D. (1982) Home range and spatial organization of coyotes in Jasper National Park, Alberta. *Journal of Wildlife Management* 46: 201-216.

Bowland, A.E. (1987) The effect of wind on small mammal trapping. *Lammergeyer* 38: 35-39.

Braithwaite, R.W. (1983) A comparison of two pitfall trap systems. *Victorian Naturalist* 100: 163-166.

Braithwaite, R.W. (1989) Shelter selection by a small mammal community in the wet-dry tropics of Australia. *Australian Mammalogy* 12: 55-59.

Breed, W.G. (1992) Reproduction of the spinifex hopping mouse (*Notomys alexis*) in the natural environment. *Australian Journal of Zoology* 40: 57-71.

Bright, P.W. & Morris, P.A. (1991) Ranging and nesting behaviour of the dormouse *Muscardinus avellanarius*, in coppice-with-stands woodland. *Journal of Zoology* (London) 226: 589-600.

Bright, P.W. & Morris, P.A. (1992) Ranging and nesting behaviour of the dormouse, *Muscardinus avellanarius*, in diverse low-growing woodland. *Journal of Zoology* (London) 224: 177-190.

Brochu, L. Caron, L. & Bergeron, J.M. (1988) Diet quality and body condition of dispersing and resident voles. *Journal of Mammalogy* 69: 704-710.

Brown, L.E. (1966) Home range and movement of small mammals. *Symposia of the Zoological Society of London* 18: 111-142.

Brown, S. & Lugo, A.E. (1990) Tropical secondary forests. *Journal of Tropical Ecology* 6: 1-31.

Brown, G.W. & Triggs, B.E. (1990) Diets of wild canids and foxes in East Gippsland 1983-1987, using predator scat anlysis. *Australina Mammalogy* 13: 209-213.

Brunner H., Amor, R.L. & Stephens, P.L. (1976) The use of predator scat analysis in a mammal survey at Dartmouth in north-eastern Victoria. *Australian Wildlife Research* 3: 85-90.

Brunner, H. & Coman, B.J. (1974) *The identification of mammalian hair.* Intaka Press, Melbourne.

Brunner, H. & Wallis, R. (1986) Roles of predator scat analysis in Australian mammal research. *Victorian Naturalist* 103: 79-87.

Burnham, K.P., Anderson, D.R. & Laake, J.L. (1980) *Estimation of denisty from line transect sampling of biological populations.* Wildlife Monograph No. 72. The Wildlife Society, Washington DC.

Buskirk, S.W. & Lindstedt, S.L. (1989) Sex biases in trapped samples of Mustelidae. *Journal of Mammalogy* 70: 88-97.

Butler, J., Roper, T.J. & Clark, A.J. (1994) Investigation of badger (*Meles meles*) setts using soil resistivity measurments. *Journal of Zoology* (London) 232: 409-418.

Canova, L. & Fasola, M. (1993) Food habits and trophic relationships of small mammals in six habitats of the northern Po plain (Italy). *Mammalia* 57: 188-199.

Cant, J.G.H. (1977) A census of the agouti (*Dasyprocta punctata*) in seasonally dry forest at Tikal, Guatemala, with some comments on strip censusing. *Journal of Mammalogy* 58: 688-690.

Carey, A.B. & Witt, J.W. (1991) Track counts as indicies of abundances of arboreal rodents. *Journal of Mammalogy* 72: 192-193.

Chabreck, R.H., Constantin, B.U. & Hamilton, R.B. (1986) Use of chemical ant repellents during small mammal trapping. *Southwestern Naturalist* 31: 109-110.

Chandrasekar-Rao, A. & Musser, G.G. (1993) New distribution record for *Mus caroli*. *Mammalia* 57: 462-463.

Charles-Dominique, P.M., Atramentowicz, M., Charles-Dominique, M., Gerard, H., Hladik, A., Hladik, C.M. & Pevost, M.F. (1981) Les mammiferes fruivores arboricoles nocturnes d'une forêt guyanaise: interrelations plantes-animaux. *Revue Ecologique (Terre et Vie)* 35: 341-435.

Chitty, D. (1937) A ringing technique for small mammals. *Journal of Animal Ecology* 6: 36-53.

Chitty, D. and Kempson, D.A. (1949) Prebaiting small mammal traps and a new design of live trap. *Ecology* 30: 356-342.

Chopra, B. & Sood,, M.L. (1984) New object and new place reactions of *Rattus meltada*. *Acta Theriologica* 29: 403-412.

Christensen, J.T. (1993) The seasonal variation in breeding and growth of *Mastomys natalensis* (Rodentia: Muridae): evidence for resource limitation. *African Journal of Ecology* 31: 1-9.

Christian, D.P. (1977) Effects of fire on small mammal populations in a desert grassland. *Journal of Mammalogy* 58:423-427.

Churchfield, S. (1990) *The Natural History of Shrews*. Christopher Helm, London.

Cittadino, E.A., de Carli, P., Busch, M. & Kravetz, F.O. (1994) Effects of food supplementation on rodents in winter. *Journal of Mammalogy* 75: 446-453.

Clark, D.A. (1980) Age- and sex-dependent foraging strategies of a small mammalian omnivore. *Journal of Animal Ecology* 49: 549-563.

Clark, W.R. (1994) Habitat selection by muskrats in experimental marshes undergoing succession. *Canadian Journal of Zoology* 72: 675-680.

Clevedon Brown, J. & Stoddart, D.M. (1977) Killing mammals and general post-mortem methods. *Mammal Review* 7: 63-94.

Cockburn, A., Fleming, M. & Wainer, J. (1978) The comparative effectiveness of drift fence pit-fall trapping and conventional cage trapping of vertebrates in the Big Desert, north-western Victoria. *Victorian Naturalist* 96: 92-95.

Coe, M.J. & Isaac, F.M. (1965) Pollination of the Baybab (*Adansonia digitata* L.) by the lesser bush baby (*Galago crassicaudatus* E. Geoffroy). *East African Wildlife Journal* 3: 123-124.

Conner, D.A. (1984) The role of an acoustic display in territorial maintenance in the pika. *Canadian Journal of Zoology* 62: 1906-1909.

Corbet, G. (1968) *Instructions for Collectors No. 1: Mammals (excluding marine mammals).* British Museum (Natural History), London.

Corlett, R.T. (1994) What is secondary forest? *Journal of Tropical Ecology* 10: 445-447.

Cowan, P.E. (1977) Systematic patrolling and orderly behaviour of rats during recovery from deprivation. *Animal Behaviour* 25: 171-184.

Cowen, P.E. & Barnett, S.A. (1975) The new-object and new-place reactions of *Rattus rattus* L. *Zoological Journal of the Linnaien Society* 56: 219-234.

Cox, T.P. (1989) Odor-based discrimination between non-contigious demes of wild Mus. *Journal of Mammalogy* 70: 549-556.

Crawford, C.S. & Seely, M.K. (1994) Detritus mass loss in the Namib desert dunefield: influence on termites, gerbiles and exposure to surface conditions. *Journal of African Zoology* 108: 49-54.

da Cunha, A. and Barnett, A. (1988) *Small Mammals-Mamiferos Pequenos.* Mammal Report No. 2, INPA-RGS-SEMA Report Series, Project Maracá.

Cuthill, I. (1991) Field experiments in animal behaviour: methods and ethics. *Animal Behaviour* 42: 1007-1014.

D'Andrea, P.S., Cerqueira, R. & Hingst, E.D. (1994) Age estimation of the gray four eyed opossum, *Philander opossum* (Didelphimorphia: Didelphidae). *Mammalia* 58: 283-291.

Davis, D.E. (1953) Analysis of home range from recapture data. *Journal of Mammalogy* 34: 252-258.

Davis, R.A. (1961) A simple live-trap for small mammals. *Proceedings of the Zoological Society London* 137: 631-633.

Davis, D.E. & Emlen, J.T. (1956) Differential trapability of rats according to size and sex. *Journal of Wildlife Management* 20: 326-327.

Dawson, T.J. & Denny, M.J.S. (1969) A bioclimatological comparison of the summer day microenvironments of two species of arid-zone kangaroo. *Ecology* 50: 328-332.

Deitz, J.M. (1983) Notes on the natural history of some Brazilian small mammals in central Brazil. *Journal of Mammalogy* 64: 521-523.

Delany, M.J. (1972) The ecology of small rodents in tropical Africa. *Mammal Review* 2: 1-42.

Delany, M.J. (1974) *The Ecology of Small Mammals*. Institute of Biology, Studies in Biology Series, No. 51. Edward Arnold, London.

Deloya, C. (1991) Una nueva especie Mexicana de aphodius (Coelotrachelus) Schmidt 1913 (Coleopter: Scarabaeidae, Aphodiinae). Asociada con *Thomomys umbrinus* (Rodentia; Geomyidae). *Folia Entomologica Mexicana* 81: 199-207.

Dempster, E.R. & Perrin, M.R. (1994) Divergence in acoustic repertoire of sympatric and allopatric gerbil species (Rodentia: Gerbillinae). *Mammalia* 58: 93-104.

Desy, E.A., Batzli, G.O. & Jike, L. (1989) Comparison of vole movements assessed by trapping and radiotracking. *Journal of Mammalogy* 70: 652-656.

Devenport, J.A. & Devenport, L.D. (1994) Spatial navigation in natural habitats by ground-dwelling sciurids. *Animal Behaviour* 47: 727-729.

Dewsbury, D.A., Estep, D.Q. & Lanier, D.L. (1977) Estrous cycles of nine species of muroid rodents. *Journal of Mammalogy* 58: 89-92.

Dickman, C.R. & Doncaster, C.P. (1987) The ecology of small mammals in urban habitats 1: populations in a patchy environment. *Journal of Applied Ecology* 56: 629-640.

Dickman, C.R. & Doncaster, C.P. (1989) The ecology of small mammals in urban habitats 2: demography and dispersal. *Journal of Applied Ecology* 58: 119-127.

Dickman, C.R., Predavec, M. & Lynam, A.J. (1991) Differential predation of size and sex class of mice by the barn owl, *Tyto alba*. *Oikos* 62: 67-76.

Doncaster, C.P. & Micol, T. (1988) Comparison of three absolute estimates of coypu abundance from cage trapping. *Acta Oecologica General* 9: 88-99.

Doucet, G.J. & Bider, J.R. (1974) The effects of weather on the activity of the masked shrew. *Journal of Mammalogy* 55: 348-363.

Douglass, R.J. (1989) The use of radiotelemetry to evaluate micro-habitat selection by deermice. *Journal of Mammalogy* 70: 643-652.

Douglass, R.J., Douglass, K.S. & Rossi, L. (1992) Ecological distribution of bank voles and wood mice in disturbed habitats: preliminary results. *Acta Theriologica* 37: 359-370.

Dowsett, R.J. (1993) The red-flanked duiker *Cephalophus rufilatus* does not occur in Congo and Gabon. *Mammalia* 57: 445-446.

Draulans, D., Perremans, K., van Vessem, J. & Pollet, M. (1987) Analysis of pellets of the grey heron, *Ardea cinerea*, from colonies in Belgium. *Journal of Zoology* (London) 211: 695-708.

Duckworth, J.W., Harrison, D.L. & Timmins, R.J. (1993) Notes on a collection of small mammals from the Ethiopian rift valley. *Mammalia* 57: 278-282.

Duckworth, A.C., Maddock, A.H. & Hickman, G.C. (1987) A live-trap for the capture of the giant golden mole. *South African Journal of Wildlife Research* 17: 17-19.

Dueser, R.D. & Shugart, H.H. (1978) Microhabitats in a forest-floor small mammal fauna. *Ecology* 59: 89-98.

Durden, L.A. (1991) Pseudoscorpions associated with mammals in Papua New Guinea. *Biotropica* 23: 204-206.

Dwyer, P.D. (1984) From garden to forest: small rodents and plant succession in Papua New Guinea. *Australian Mammalogy* 7: 29-36.

Eberhardt, L.L. (1978) Transect methods for population studies. *Journal of Wildlife Management* 42: 1-31.

Ecke, D.H. & Kinney, A.R. (1956) Aging meadow mice, *Microtus californicus*, by observation of molt progression. *Journal of Mammalogy* 37: 249-254.

Ellison, G.T.H. (1993) Group size, burrow structure and hoarding activity of pouched mice (*Saccostomus campestris*: Cricetidae) in southern Africa. *African Journal of Ecology* 31: 135-155.

Emamdie, D. & Warren, J. (1993) Varietal taste preference for cacao *Therobroma cacao* L. by the Neotropical red squirrel *Sciurus granatensis* (Humboldt). *Biotropica* 25: 365-368.

Emlen, J.T. (1971) Population densities of birds derived from transect counts. *Auk* 88: 323-342.

Emlen, J.T., Hine, R.L., Fuller, W.A. & Alfonso, P. (1957) Dropping boards for population studies of small mammals. *Journal of Wildlife Management* 21: 300-314.

Emmons, L.H. (1981) Morphological, ecological, and behavioral adaptions for arboreal browsing in *Dactylomys dactylinus* (Rodentia, Echimyidae). *Journal of Mammalogy* 62: 183-189.

Emmons, L.H. (1984) Geographic variation in densities and diversities of non-flying mammals in Amazonia. *Biotropica* 16: 210-222.

Emmons, L.H. (1993) A new genus and species of rat from Borneo (Rodentia: Muridae). *Proceedings of the Biological Society of Washington* 106: 752-761.

Epple, G., Mason, J.R., Nolte, D.L. & Campbell, D.L. (1993) Effects of predator odors on feeding in the mountain beaver (*Aplodontia rufa*). *Journal of Mammalogy* 74: 715-722.

Erickson, A.B. (1947) A multiple type rat and mouse holder. *Journal of Wildlife Management* 11: 351.

Erlinge, S. (1967) Home range of the otter *Lutra lutra* L. in southern Sweden. *Oikos* 18: 186-209.

Fa, J.E., Lopez-Paniagua, J., Romero, F.J., Gomez, J.L. & Lopez, J.C. (1990) Influence of habitat charactersistics on small mammals in a Mexican high-altitude grassland. *Journal of Zoology* (London) 221-275-292.

Fairley, J.S. (1982) Short term effects of rining and toe-clipping on the recapture of Wood mice (*Apodemus sylvaticus*). *Journal of Zoology* (London) 197: 295-297.

Fasola, M., Barbieri, F. & Canova, L. (1993) Test of an electronic individual tag for newts. *Herpetological Journal* 3: 149-150.

Feinsinger, P., Spears, E.E. & Poole, R.W. (1981) A simple measure of niche breadth. *Ecology* 62: 27-32.

Feldhamer, G.A., Klann, R.S., Gerard, A.S. & Driskell, A.C. (1993) Habitat partitioning, body size, and timing of parturition in pygmy shrews and associated sorcids. *Journal of Mammalogy* 74: 403-411.

Feldhamer, G.A. & Stober, T.L. (1993) Dental anomalies in five species of North American shrews. *Mammalia* 57: 115-121.

Fisher, M. (1991) A reappraisal of the reproductive ecology of *Arvicanthis* in Africa. *African Journal of Ecology* 29: 17-27.

Fitzgibbon, C.D. & Rathbun, G.B. (1994) Surveying *Rhynchocyon* elephant-shrews in tropical forest. *African Journal of Ecology* 32: 50-57.

Flannery, T.F. & Schouten, P. (1994) *Possums of the World*. Geo Productions and the Australian Museum, Sydney.

Fleming, T.H. (1971) *Population ecology of three species of neotropical rodents*. Miscellaneous Publications of the Museum of Zoology, Michigan No. 143.

Fleming, T.H. (1973) Aspects of the population dynamics of three species of opossums in the Panama canal zone. *Journal of Mammalogy* 53: 619-623.

Flowerdew, J.R. (1976) Techniques in Mammalogy. Chapter Four. Ecological Methods. *Mammal Review* 6: 123-159.

Fox, B. & Powell, R. (1985) Niche spaces and small mammal comminities. *Australian Mammalogy* 8 (3).

Franklin, W.L. & El-Absy, A. (1985) Application of freeze-marking to wildlife in the field: prarie dogs. *Proceedings of the Iowa Academy of Science* 93: 44-47.

French, J., Latham, D.M., Oldham, R.S. & Bullock, D.J. (1992) An automated radio-tracking system for use with amphibians. In Pried, I.G. & Swift, S.M. (eds.) *Wildlife Telemetry remote monitoring and tracking of animals*. pp477-483. Ellis Horwood, New York.

Freudenberger, D.O. (1992) Gut capacity, functional allocation of gut volume and size distributions of digesta particles in two Macropodid Marsupials (*Macropus robustus robustus* and *M. r. erubescens*) and the feral goat (*Capra hircus*). *Australian Journal of Zoology* 40: 551-561.

Friend, G.R. (1978) A comparison of predator scat analysis with conventional techniques in a mammal survey of contrasting habitats in Gippsland, Victoria. *Australian Wildlife Research* 5: 75-83.

Friend, G.R. (1984) Relative efficiency of two pitfall-drift fence systems for sampling small vertebrates. *The Australian Zoologist* 21: 423-433.

Fullagar, P.J. & Jewell, P.A. (1965) Marking small rodents and the difficulties of using leg rings. *Journal of Zoology* (London) 147: 224-228.

Fuller, W.A. (1988) Is weight a reliable index to age in microtine rodents? *Acta Theriologica* 33: 247-261.

Gardner, R.A., Molyneaux, D.H. & Stebbings, R.E. (1987) Studies of the prevalence of heamatozoa of British bats. *Mammal Review* 17: 75-80.

Gardner, A.L. & Romo, M.R. (1993) A new *Thomasomys* (Mammalia: Rodentia) from the Peruvian Andes. *Proceedings of the Biological Society of Washington* 106: 762-774.

Gates, C.A. & Tanner, G.W. (1988) Effects of prescribed burning on herbaceous vegetation and pocket gopher (*Geomys pinetis*) in a sandhill community. *Florida Scientist* 51: 129-139.

Gates, C.A., Tanner, G.W. & Gates, B.K. (1988) A modified live trap for the capture of southeastern pocket gophers. *Florida Scientist* 51: 156-158.

Gatz, A.J. (1981) Morphologically inferred niche differentiation in stream fishes. *American Naturalist* 106: 10-21.

Gebczynska, Z. & Myrcha, A. (1966) The method of quantitative determining of the food composition of rodents. *Acta Theriologica* 16: 385-390.

Gérard, D., Bauchau, V. & Smets, S. (1994) Reduced trappability in wild mice, *Mus musculus domesticus*, heterozygous for Robertsonian translocations. *Animal Behaviour* 47: 877-883.

Gettinger, R.D. (1975) Metabolism and thermoregulation of a fossorial rodent, the northern pocket gopher (*Thomomys talpoides*). *Physiological Zoology* 48: 311-322.

Getz, L.L. (1968) Influence of weather on the activity of the red-backed vole. *Journal of Mammalogy* 49: 565-570.

Geuse, P., Bachau, V. & Le Boulenge, E. (1985) Distribution and population dynamics of bank voles and wood mice in a patchy woodland habitat in central Belgium. *Acta Zoologica Fennica* 173: 65-68.

Gliwicz, J. (1993) Dispersal in bank voles: benefits to emigrants or to residents? *Acta Theriologica* 38: 31-38.

Goldingay, R.L. (1994) Loud calls of the yellow-bellied glider, *Petaurus australis*: territorial behaviour by an arboreal marsupial? *Australian Journal of Zoology* 42: 279-293.

Goldingay, R.L. & Denny, M.J.S. (1986) Capture-related aspects of the ecology of *Antechinus flavipes* (Marsupialia: Dasyuridae). *Australian Mammalogy* 9: 131-133.

Goldingay, R.L. & Kavanagh, R.P. (1988) Detectability of the feathertail glider, *Acrobates pygmaeus* (Marsupialia: Burramyidae), in relation to measured weather variables. *Australian Mammalogy* 11: 67-70.

Goodman, D. (1984) *Statistics of reproductive rate estimates and their implications for population protection*. Report of the International Whaling Commission, Special Issue No. 6: 161-173.

Gorden, R.D. & Howden, H.F. (1973) Five new species of Mexican *Aphodius* (Coleoptera: Scarabaeidae) associated with *Thomomys umbrinus* (Geomyidae). *Annals of the Entomological Society of America* 6: 436-443.

Gorman, M.R., Ferkin, M.H., Nelson, R.J. & Zucker, I. (1993) Reproductive status influences odor preferences of the meadow vole, *Microtus pennsylvanicus*, in winter day lengths. *Canadian Journal of Zoology* 71: 1748-1754.

Goyal, S.P. & Ghosh, P.K. (1993) Burrow structure of two gerbil species of Thar desert, India. *Acta Theriologica* 38: 453-356.

Granjon, L. & Duplantier, J. (1993) Social structure in sympatric populations of a murid rodent *Mastomys natalensis* in Sénégal. *Acta Theriologica* 38: 39-47.

Grant, W.E., Birney, E.C., French, N.R. & Swift, D.M. (1982) Structure and productivity of grassland small mammal communities related to grazing-induced changes in vegetation cover. *Journal of Mammalogy* 63: 248-260.

Groombridge, B. (Ed.)(1993) *1994 IUCN Red List of Threatened Animals*. IUCN, Gland, Switzerland.

Gurnell, J. (1977) Neutral cage behaviour interaction in wild wood mice, *Apodemus sylvaticus* (Linne, 1758). *Saugetierkundliche Mitteilungen* 33: 57-66.

Gurnell, J. (1980) The effects of prebaiting live traps on catching woodland rodents. *Acta Theriologica* 25: 255-264.

Gurnell, J. & Flowerdew, J.R. (1990) *Live Trapping Small Mammals: A Practical Guide.* Occasional Publications of the Mammal Society No. 3. The Mammal Society, Reading.

Gurnell, J. & Langbein, J.(1983) Effects of trap position on the capture of woodland rodents. *Journal of Zoology* (London) 200: 289-292.

Guthrie, D.R., Osborne, J.C. & Mosby, H.S. (1967) Physiological changes associated with shock in confined gray squirrels. *Journal of Wildlife Management* 31: 102-108.

Hagen, A., Stenseth, N.C., Ostbye, E. & Skar, H.-J. (1980) The eye lens as an age indicator in the root vole. *Acta Theriologica* 25: 39-50.

Hall, E.R. & Russell, W.C. (1933) *Dermestes* beetles as an aid to cleaning bones. *Journal of Mammalogy* 14: 372-374.

Hall, J.B. & Okali, D.U.U. (1978) Observer-bias in a floristic survey of complex tropical vegetation. *Journal of Ecology* 66: 241-249.

Haila, Y. & Kouki, J. (1994) The phenomenon of biodiversity in conservation biology. *Annals. Zoologici. Fennici* 31: 5-18.

Hamilton, W.J. (1941) The food of small forest mammals in eastern United States. *Journal of Mammalogy* 22: 250-263.

Hanna, N. & Anderson, J. (1993) *Assessing the Status and Distribution of the Black-and-Rufus Elephant shrew.* Unpublished expedition report of the Oxford University Njule '92 Expedition.

Hansson, L. (1970) Methods of morphological diet micro-analysis in rodents. *Oikos* 21: 255-266.

Hansson, L. (1975) Comparison between small mammal sampling with small and large removal quadrats. *Oikos* 26: 398-404.

Hansson, L. & Hoffmeyer, I. (1973) Snap and live trap efficiency for small mammals. *Oikos* 24: 477-478.

Hardy. R., Quy, R.J. & Huson, L.W. (1983) Estimation of age in the Norway rat (*Rattus norvegicus* Berkenhout) from the weight of the eyelens. *Journal of Applied Ecology* 20: 97-102.

Harper, S.J., Bollinger, E.K. & Barret, G.W. (1993) Effects of habitat patch shape on population dynamics of meadow voles (*Microtus pennsyvanicus*). *Journal of Mammalogy* 74: 1045-1055.

Harris, S., Cresswell, W.J., Forde, P.G., Trewhella, W.J., Woollard, T. & Wray, S. (1990) Home-range analysis using radio-tracking data - a review of problems and techniques particularly as applied to the study of mammals. *Mammal Review* 20: 97-123.

Harrison, D.L. (1972) *The Mammals of Arabia.* Ernest Benn, London.

Hawes, M.L. (1977) Home range, territoriality, and ecological separation in sympatric shrews, *Sorex vagrans* and *Sorex obscurus*. *Journal of Mammalogy* 58: 354-367.

Hawkins, C.E. & Macdonald, D.W. (1992) A spool-and-line method for investigating the movements of badgers, *Meles meles*. *Mammalia* 56: 322-325.

Hayes, J.P. & Cross, S.P. (1987) Characteristics of logs used by western redbacked voles, *Clethrionomys californicus* and deer mice, *Peromyscus maniculatus*. *Canadian Field Naturalist* 101: 543-546.

Hayes, J.P. & Richmond, M.E. (1993) Clinal variation and morphology of woodrats (*Neotoma*) of the eastern United States. *Journal of Mammalogy* 74: 204-216.

Hayne, D.W. (1949) Two methods for estimating population from trapping records. *Journal of Mammalogy* 30: 399-411.

Hearney, A.W. & Jennings, T.J.(1983) Annual foods of the red deer (*Cervus elaphus*) and the roe deer (*Capreolus capreolus*) in the east of England). *Journal of Zoology* (London) 201:565-570.

Heezen, K.L. & Tester, J.R. (1967) Evaluation of radio-tracking by triangulation with special reference to deer movements. *Journal of Wildlife Management* 31: 124-141.

Heim de Balsac, H. & Hutterer, R. (1982) Les Soricidae (Mammiferes Insectivores) des îsles du Golfe du Guinée: faits nouveaux et problemes biogéographiques. *Bonn Zool Beitr* 33: 133-150.

Henry, par O. (1994) Saisons de reproduction chez trois Rongeurs et un Artiodactyle en Guyane fraçaise, en fonction des facteurs du milieu et de l'alimentation. *Mammalia* 58: 183-200.

Henttonen, H., Hansson, L. & Saitoh, T. (1992) Rodent dynamics and community structure: *Clethrionomys rufocanus* in northern Fennoscandia and Hokkaido. *Annals. Zoologici. Fennici* 29: 1-6.

Heske, E.J. (1987) Responses of a population of California voles, *Microtus californicus,* to odor-baited traps. *Journal of Mammalogy* 68:64-72.

Hespenheide, H.A. (1973) Ecological inferences from morphological data. *Annual Revue of Ecology and Systematics* 4: 213-229.

Hickman, G.C. (1979) A live-trap and trapping technique for fossorial mammals. *South African Journal of Zoology* 14: 9-12.

Hofmann, R.R. (1983) Adaptive changes of gastric and intestinalmorphology in responce to different fibre content in ruminant diets. *Bulletin of the Royal Society of New Zealand* 20: 51-58.

Hogan, K.M., Hedin, M.C., Koh, H.S., Davis, S.K. & Greenbaum, I.F. (1993) Systematic and taxonomic implications of karyotypic, electrophoretic, and mitochondrial-DNA variation in *Peromyscus* from the Pacific northwest. *Journal of Mammalogy* 74:819-831.

Holbrook, S.J. (1982) Ecological inferences from mandibular morphology of Peromyscus maniculatus. *Journal of Mammalogy* 63: 399-408.

Honacki, J.H., Kinman, K.E. & Koeppl, J.W. (1982) *Mammal Species of the World: A Taxonomic and Geographical Reference*. Allan Press & Association of Systematics, Collins.

van Horn, B. (1982). Niches of adult and juvenile deer mice (*Peromyscus maniculatus*) in seral stages of coniferous forest. *Ecology* 63: 992-1003.

Hoodless, A. & Morris, P.A. (1993) An estimate of population density of the fat dormouse (*Glis glis*). *Journal of Zoology* (London) 230: 337-340.

Hooper, E.T. (1950) Use dermestid beetles instead of cooking pots. *Journal of Mammalogy* 31: 100-102.

Horacek, I. (1984) Reliability of the marking-recapture data - a testing method. *Lynx* (Prague) 22: 88.

Hume, I.D., Jazwinski, E. & Flannery, T.F. (1993) Morphology and function of the digestive tract in New Guinean possums. *Australian Journal of Zoology* 41: 85-100.

Hurst, J.L. (1988) A system for the individual recognition of small rodents at a distance, used in free-living and enclosed populations of house mice. *Journal of Zoology* (London) 215: 363-367.

Hurst, J.P. (1989) The complex network of olfactory communication in populations of wild house mice, *Mus domesticus* Rutty: urine marking and investigation within family groups. *Animal Behaviour* 37: 705-725.

Hurst,J.L., Fang, J. & Barnard, C. (1994) The role of substrate odours in maintaining social tolerance between male house mice, *Mus musculus domesticus*: relatedness, incidental kinship effects and the establishment of social status. *Animal Behaviour* 48: 157-167.

Iskjaer, C., Slade, N.A. Childs, J.E., Glass, G.E. & Korch, G.W. (1989) Body mass as a measure of body size in small mammals. *Journal of Mammalogy* 70: 662-667.

Jaksic, F.M. & Yanez, J.L. (1979) The diet of the barn owl in central Chile and its relation to availability of prey. *Auk* 96: 619-621.

James, D.A. & Lockerd, M.J. (1986) Refinement of the Shugart-Patten-Dueser model for analysing ecological niche patterns. In Verner, J., Morrison, M.L. & Ralph, C.J. (eds.) *Wildlife 2000: Modeling Habitat Relationships of Terrestrial Vertebrates*. pp. 51-56. University of Wisconsin Press.

Janson, C.H., Terborgh, J. & Emmons, L.H. (1981) Non-flying mammals as pollinating agebts in the Amazonian forest. *Biotopica* 13: 1-6 (supplement).

Jeanmaire-Besancon, F. (1986) Estimation de l'age et de la longevite chez *Crocidura russula* (Insectivora: Soricidae). *Acta Oecologica* Applicata 7: 355-366.

Jedrzejewski, W., Jedrzejewska, B. & McNeish, E. (1992) Hunting success of the weasel *Mustela nivalis* and escape tactics of forest rodents in Bialowieza National Park. *Acta Theriologica* 37: 319-328.

Jennings, T.J. (1979) A simple technique for the production of reference slides in the study of herbivore diets by faecal analysis. *Journal of Zoology* (London) 188: 296-298.

Jett, D. & Nichols, J.D. (1987) A field comparison of nested grid and trapping web density estimators. *Journal of Mammalogy* 68: 888-892.

Jike, L., Batzli, G.O. & Getz, L.L. (1988) Home ranges of prarie voles as determined by radiotracking and powdertracking. *Journal of Mammalogy* 69: 183-186.

Johns, A.D. (1079) A comparative assessment of methods of individual tracking within a population of *Microtus agrestis* (Mammalia: Muridae). *Journal of Zoology* (London) 189: 333-338.

Johnston, R.E. & Jernigan, P. (1994) Golden hamsters recognize individuals, not just individual scents. *Animal Behaviour* 48: 129-136.

Jones, E.N. (1983) A comparison of meadow vole home ranges derived from grid trapping and radiotelemetry. *Journal of Wildlife Management* 47: 558-561.

Jones, W.T. (1989) Dispersal distance and the range of nightly movements in Merriam's Kangaroo Rats. *Journal of Mammalogy* 70: 27-34.

Justice, K.E. (1961) A new method for measuring home range of small mammals. *Journal of Mammalogy* 55: 309-318.

Kam, M. & Degen, A.A. (1994) Body mass at birth and growth rate of fat sand rat (*Psammomys obesus*) pups: effects of litter size and water content of *Atriplex halimus* consumed by pregnant and lactating females. *Functional Ecology* 8: 351-357.

Kapila, S. & Lyon, F. (1994) *Expedition Field Techniques: People Orientated Research.* Expedition Advisory Centre, London.

Kataev, G.D., Suomela, J. & Palokangas, P. (1994) Densities of microtine rodents along a pollution gradient from a copper-nickel smelter. *Oecologia* 97: 491-498.

Kaufman, G.A. (1989) Use of flourescent pigments to study social interactions in a small nocturnal rodent, *Peromyscus maniculatus*. *Journal of Mammalogy* 70: 171-174.

Kaufman, G.A. & Kaufman, D.W. (1988) Two deer mice captured simultaneously in a museum special snap trap. *Prarie Naturalist* 20: 175-176.

Kaufman, G.A. & Kaufman, D.W. (1994) Changes in body mass related to capture in the prairie deer mouse (*Peromyscus maniculatus*). *Journal of Mammalogy* 75: 681-691.

Kenward, R.(1987) *Wildlife Radio Tagging*. Academic Press, London.

Kerle, J.A. & Howe, C.J. (1992) The breeding biology of a tropical possum, *Trichosurus vulpecula arnhemensis* (Phalangeridae: Marsupialia). *Australian Journal of Zoology* 40: 653-665.

Keshava Bhat, S. & Sujatha, A. (1987) Relative efficiency of two live traps in capturing small mammals in coconut-cocoa mixed habitat. *Journal of Plant Crops* 15: 140-142.

Kierulff, M.C., Stallings, J.R. & Sabato, E.L. (1991) A method to capture the bamboo rat (*Kannabateomys amblyonyx*) in bamboo forests. *Mammalia* 55: 633-625.

King, C.M. (1991) A review of age determination methods for the stoat *Mustela erminea*. *Mammal Review* 21: 31-49.

Kinnear, J.E., Bromilow, R.N., Onus, M.L. & Sokolowski, R.E.S. (1988) The Bromilow trap: A new risk-free soft trap suitable for small to medium-sized macropods. *Australian Wildlife Research* 15: 235-237.

Kolb, H.H. (1991) Use of burrows and movements by wild rabbits (*Oryctolagus cuniculus*) on an area of sand dunes. *Journal of Applied Ecology* 28: 879-891.

Kompanje, E.J.O. & de Vries, G. TH. (1992) An almost toothless badger *Meles meles*. *Lutra* 35: 40-43.

Korn, H. (1986) Changes in home range size during growth and maturation of the wood mouse (*Apodemus sylvaticus*) and bank vole (*Clethrionomys glariolus*). *Oecologia* 68: 623-628.

Kostelecka-Myrcha, A. & Myrcha, A. (1964a) Choice of indicator in the investigation of the passage of foodstuffs through the ailementary tract of rodents. *Acta Theriologica* 9: 55-65.

Kostelecka-Myrcha, A. & Myrcha, A. (1964b) Rate of passage of foodstuffs through the ailementary tract of *Neomys fodiens* (Pennant, 1771) under laboratory conditions. *Acta Theriologica* 9: 371-373.

Kotler, B.P., Brown, J.S. & Mitchell, W.A. (1993) Environmental factors affecting patch use in two species of gerbilline rodents. *Journal of Mammalogy* 74: 614-620.

Kozakiewicz, A. & Boniecki, P. (1994) Intra- and interspecific behaviours in bank vole and striped-field mouse under enclosed conditions. *Acta Theriologica* 39: 29-36.

Krebs, C.J. (1989) *Ecological Methodology*. Harper Collins, New York.

Krebs, C.J. & Singleton, G.R. (1993) Indices of condition for small mammals. *Australian Journal of Zoology* 41: 317-323.

Kress, W.J., Schatz, G.E., Andrianifahanana, M. & Morland, H.S. (1994) Pollination of *Ravenala madagascariensis* (Strelitziaceae) by lemas in Madagascar: evidence for an archaic coevolutionary system? *American Journal of Botany* 81: 542-551.

Kryltzov, A.I. (1964) Moult and topography of Microtinae, other rodents and lagomorphs. *Z. Säugetierkunde* 29: 1-17.

Kutuzov, H. & Sicher, H. (1952) Anatomy and function of the palate in the white rat. *Anatomical Record* 114: 67-84.

Lair, H. (1990) The calls of the red squirrel: a contextual analysis of cunction. *Behaviour* 115: 254-282.

Lawrence, M.J. & Brown, R.W. (1973) *Mammals of Britain: their Tracks, Trails and Signs*. Blandford Press, London.

Laurance, W.F. (19??) Effects of weather on marsupial folivore activity in in a north Queensland upland tropical rainforest. *Australian Mammalogy* 13: 41-47.

Layne, J.N. (1987) An enclosure for protecting small mammal traps from disturbance. *Journal of Mammalogy* 68: 666-668.

Lee, J.E., White, G.C., Garrot, R.A., Bartmann, R.M. & Allredge, A.W. (1985) Accessing accuracy of a radiotelemetry system for estimating animal locations. *Journal of Wildlife Management* 49: 658-663.

Leirs, H., Stuyck, J., Verhagen, R. & Verheyen, W. (1990) Seasonal variation in growth of *Mastomys natalensis* (Rodentia: Muridae) in Morogoro, Tanzania. *African Journal of Ecology* 28: 298-306.

Lemen, C.A. & Freeman, P.W. (1985) Tracking mammals with fluorescent pigments: a new technique. *Journal of Mammalogy* 66: 134-136.

Lenders, A., Gubbels, R. & van Gelder, J.J. (1986) Thermosensitive radiotelemetry as a method to study the common hamster, *Cricetus cricetus* (L., 1758). *Lutra* 29: 261-267.

Leo, M.L. & Gardner, A.L. (1993) A new species of a giant *Thomamsomys* (Mammalia: Muridae: Sigmodontinae) from the Andes of northcentral Peru. *Proceedings of the Biological Society of Washington* 106: 417-428.

Leopold, J.H. & Calkins, L. (1951) Age changes in the Wistar albino rat eye. *American Journal of Ophtalmol.* 34: 1735-1741.

Lidicker, W.Z. (1989) *Rodents a World Survey of Species of Conservation Concern.* Occasional papers of the IUCN Species Survival Commission No. 4, IUCN, Gland, Switzerland.

Lidicker, W.Z. & Laurance, W.F. (1990) Field identification of sympatric *Rattus* (Rodentia: Muridae) in north Queensland rainforest. *Australian Mammalogy* 13: 55-56.

Lightfoot, V.M.A. & Wallis, S.J. (1982) Predation of small mammals inside Longworth traps by a weasel. *Journal of Zoology* (London) 198: 521.

Ligtvot, W. & van Wigngaarden, A. (1994) The colonisation of the island off Noord-Beveland (The Netherlands) by the common vole *Microtus arvalis*, and its consequences for the root vole *Microtus oeconomus. Lutra* 37: 1-28.

Lindenmayer, D.B. & Cunningham, R.B., Tanton, M.T. & Nix, H.A. (1991) Aspects of the use of den trees by arboreal and scansorial Marsupials inhabiting montane ash forests in Victoria. *Australian Journal of Zoology* 39: 57-65.

Linhart, S.B. & Knowlton, F.F. (1975) Determining relative abundance of coyotes by scent station lines. *Wildlife Society Bulletin* 3: 119-124.

Liro, A. (1974) Renewal of burrows by the common vole as the indicator of its numbers. *Acat Theriologica* 19: 259-272.

Lockard, R.B. & Owings, D.H. (1974a) Moon-related surface avtivity of bannertail (*Dipodomys spectabilis*) and fresno (*D. nitratoides*) kangaroo rats. *Animal Behaviour* 22: 262-273.

Lockard, R.B. & Owings, D.H. (1974b) Seasonal variation in moonlight avoidance by bannertail kangaroo rats. *Journal of Mammalogy* 55: 189-193.

Lockard, R.B. & Owings, D.H. (1974c) Seasonal change in the activity pattern of Dipodomys spectabilis. *Journal of Mammalogy* 55: 1201-1219.

Lockie, J.D. & Day, M.G. (1964) The use of anaesthesia in the handling of stoats and weasels. In Graham-Jones, O. (ed) *Small Mammal Anaesthesia.* pp. 187-189. Pergamon Press, Oxford.

Loeb, S.C. & Schwab, R.G. (1989) An evaluation of three methods for determining diet quality of free-ranging small herbivorous mammals. *Canadian Journal of Zoology* 67: 96-102.

Loft, E.R., Menke, J.W. & Burton, T.S. (1984) Seasonal movements and summer habitats of female black-tailed deer. *Journal of Wildlife Management* 48: 1317-1325.

Lomolino, M.V. (1994) Species richness of mammals inhabiting nearshore archipelagoes: area, isolation, and immigration filters. *Journal of Mammalogy* 75: 39-49.

López-Fuster, M.J. & Ventura, J. (1992) Relative growth and annual size variation in *Crocidura russula* from Ebro Delta, Spain. *Acta Theriologica* 37: 371-380.

Lord, R.D. (1959) The lens as an indicator of age in cottontail rabbits. *Journal of Wildlife Management* 23: 358-360.

Lord, R.D., Vilches, A.M., Maiztegui, J.I. & Soldini, C.A. (1970) The tracking board: a relative census technique for studying rodents. *Journal of Mammalogy* 51: 828-829.

Luff, M.L. (1975) Some features influencing the efficiency of pitfall traps. *Oecologia* (Berlin) 19: 345-357.

Lumer, C. (1980) Rodent pollination of Blakea (Melastomataceae) in a Costa Rican cloudforest. *Brittonia* 32: 512-517.

Mabberly, D.J. (1983) *Tropical Rain Forest Ecology*. Blackie & Sons, Oxford.

Madsen, R.M. (1967) *Age determination of wildlife - a bibliography*. US Department of the Interior, Washington DC.

Malcolm, J.R. (1991) Comparitive abundances of Neotropical small mammals by trap height. *Journal of Mammalogy* 72: 188-191.

Malhi, C.S. & Parshad, V.R. (1994) Responses of *Bandicota bengalensis* to below ground baiting in orchard. *Mammalia* 58: 73-84.

Maly, M.S. & Cranford, J.A. (1985) Relative capture efficiency of large and small sherman live traps. *Acta Theriologica* 30: 161-165.

Mankin, P.C. & Getz, L.L. (1994) Burrow morphology as related to social organisation of *Microtus ochrogaster*. *Journal of Mammalogy* 75: 492-99.

Mares, M.A. & Genoways, H.H. (1982) *Mammalian Biology in South America*. Pymatuning Laboratory of Ecology, Special Publication No. 6.

Martin, G.G.(1972) Censusing mouse populations by means of tracking. *Ecology* 53: 859-867.

Martinsson, B., Hansson, L. & Angelstam, P. (1993) Small mammal dynamics in adjacent landscapes with varying predator communities. *Annals Zoologici Fennici* 30: 31-42.

Masser, M.P. & Grant, W.E. (1986) Fire ant induced trap mortality of small mammals in east-central Texas. *Southwestern Naturalist* 31: 540-542.

Matson, J.O. (1982) Numerical analysis of rodent distributional patterns in Zacatecas, Mexico. *Journal of Mammalogy* 63: 73-84.

McClearn, D., Kohler, J., McGowan, K.J., Cedeno, E., Carbone, L.G. & Miller, D. (1994) Arboreal and terrestrial mammal trapping on Gigante

Peninsula, Barro Colorado Nature Monument, Panama. *Biotropica* 26: 208-213.

McCabe, T.R. & Elison, G. (1986) An effective live-capture technique for muskrat. *Wildlife Society Bulletin* 14: 282-284.

McPhee, E.C. (1988) Ecology and diet of some rodents from the lower montane region of Papua New Guinea. *Australian Wildlife Research* 15: 91-102.

Mengak, M.T. & Guynn, D.C. (1987) Pitfall and snap-traps for sampling small mammals and herpetofauna. *American Midland Naturalist* 118: 284-288.

Michener, G.R. (1993) Lethal myiasis of Richardson's ground squirrels by the sarcophagid fly *Neobellieria citellivora*. *Journal of Mammalogy* 74: 148-155.

Mihok, S. (1984) Life history profiles of boreal meadow voles (*Microtus pennsylvanicus*). *Special Publications of the Carnegie Natural History Museum*, No. 10: 91-102.

Miles, M.A., de Souza, A.A. & Povoa, M.M. (1981) Mammal tracking and nest location in Brazilian forest with an improved spool-and-line device. *Journal of Zoology* (London) 195: 331-347.

Miller, L.M. & Anderson, S. (1977) Bodily proportions of Uruguayan myomorph rodents. *American Museum Novitates* 2615: 1-10.

Mitchell, A. (1982) *Reaching the Rainforest Roof*. Leeds Philosophical and Literary Society for the Global Environmental Monitoring System and the Royal Geographical Society, London.

Mitchell-Jones, A.J. (ed.) (1987) *The Bat Worker's Manual*. Nature Conservation Council, Peterborough.

Montgomery, W.I. (1979) Multiple captures in Longworth traps. *Journal of Zoology* (London) 188: 286-288.

Montgomery, W.I. (1980a) The use of arboreal runways by woodland rodents, *Apodemus sylvaticus* (L.), *A. flavicollis* (Melchior) and *Clethrionomys glareolus* (Schreber). *Mammal Review* 10: 189-195.

Montgomery, W.I. (1980b) Mortality of small rodents captured in live-traps. *Acta Theriologica* 25: 277-294.

Montgomery, W.I. (1985) The effect of marking on recapture and the estimation of populations of *Apodemus* spp. *Journal of Zoology* (London) 206: 267-269.

Montgomery, W.I. (1987) The application of capture-mark-recapture methods to the enumeration of small mammal populations *Symposium of the Zoological Society of London*, No. 58: 25-57.

Morris, D. (1962) The behaviour of the Green Acoughi (*Myoprocta pratti*) with special reference to scatter hoarding. *Proceedings of the Zoology Society of London* 139: 701-732.

Morris, P.A. (1988) A study of home range and movements in the hedgehog (*Erinaceus europaeus*) *Journal of Zoology* (London) 214: 433-449.

Morris, R.D. (1968) A comparison of capture success between Sherman and Longworth live traps. *Canadian Field-Naturalist* 82: 84-87.

Morris, P.A. & Hoodless, A. (1992) Movements and hibernaculum site in the fat dormouse (*Glis glis*). *Journal of Zoology (London)* 228: 685-687.

Morris, P. & Whitebread, S. (1986) A method for trapping the dormouse (*Muscardinus avellanarius*). *Journal of Zoology* (London) 210: 642-644.

Morris, P. & Wroot, S. (1985) *Preparation of Mammal Skins for Scientific, Educational and Display Purposes.* Occasional Publications of the Mammal Society, No. 7. The Mammal Society, Bristol.

Mukherjee, S., Goyal, S.P. & Chellam, R. (1994) Standardisation of scat analysis techniques for leopard (*Panthera pardus*) in Gir National Park, western India. *Mammalia* 58: 139-143.

Mullican, T.R. (1988) Radio telemetry and flourescent pigments: a comparison of techniques. *Journal of Wildlife Management* 52: 627-631.

Murie, J.O. (1977) Cues used for cache-finding by agoutis (Dasyprocta punctata). *Journal of Mammalogy* 58: 95-96.

Murua, R., Gonzalez, L.A. & Jofre, C. (1980) Experimental food preferences of two southern Chilean rodents. *Journal of Mammalogy* 61: 138-140.

Myers, G.T. & Vaughan, T.A. (1964) Food habits of the plains pocket gopher in eastern Colorado. *Journal of Mammalogy* 45: 588-598.

Myrcha, A. (1964) Variations in the length and weight of the ailimentary tract of *Clethrionomys glariolus* (Schreber, 1780). *Acta Theriologica* 10: 139-148.

Mystkowska, E.T. & Sidorowicz, J. (1961) Influence of the weather on captures of micromammalia. II Insectivora. *Acta Theriologica* 5: 263-273.

Nagorsen, D.W. & Peterson, R.L. (1980) *Mammal Collectors Manual: a guide for collecting, documenting, and preparing mammal specimens for scientific research.* Royal Ontario Museum Publications in Life Sciences, Toronto.

Neal, B.R. & Cock, A.G. (1969) An analysis of the selection of small African mammals by two break-back traps. *Journal of Zoology* (London) 158: 335-340.

Neff, D.J. (1968) The pellet-group count technique for big game trend, census, and distribution: a review. *Journal of Wildlife Management* 32: 597-614.

Negus, N.C., Berger, P.J. & Forslund, L.G. (1977) Reproductive strategy of *Microtus montanus*. *Journal of Mammalogy* 58: 347-353.

Nichols, J.D. (1986) On the use of enumeration estimators for intra-specific comparisons, with comments on a 'trappability' estimator. *Journal of Mammalogy* 67: 590-593.

Nicoll, M.E. & Rathbun, G.B. (1990) *African Insectivora and Elephant-Shrews an Action Plan for their Conservation*. IUCN, Gland.

Norbury, G.L. (1988a) Microscopic analysis of herbivore diets - a problem and a solution. *Australian Wildlife Research* 15: 51-57.

Norbury, G.L. (1988b) A comparison of stomach and faecal samples for diet analysis of grey kangaroos. *Australian Wildlife Research* 15: 249-255.

Norbury, G.L. & Sanson, G.D. (1992) Problems with measuring diet selection of terrestrial mammalian herbivores. *Australian Journal of Ecology* 17: 1-7.

Norton, T.W. (1986) Notes on the size of *Pseudomys novaehollandiae* (Waterhouse) (Rodentia: Muridae) in Tasmania. *Australian Mammalogy* 9: 61-62.

Norton, T.W. (1987) The effect of trap placement on trapping success of *Rattus lutreolus velutinus* (Thomas) (Muridae: Rodentia) in north-east Tasmania. *Australian Wildlife Research* 14: 305-310.

Nowak, R.M. (1991a) *Walker's Mammals of the World* Volume 1. The Johns Hopkins University Press, Baltimore.

Nowak, R.M. (1991b) *Walker's Mammals of the World* Volume 2. The Johns Hopkins University Press, Baltimore.

Ochoa, J., Soriano, P.J., Lew, D. & Ojeda, M.C. (1993) Taxonomic and distributional notes on some bates and rodents from Venezuela. *Mammalia* 57: 393-400.

O'Farrell, M.J., Clark, W.A., Emmerson, F.H., Juarez, S.M., Kay, F.R., O'Farrell, T.M. & Goodlett, T.Y. (1994) Use of a mesh live trap for small mammals: are results from Sherman live traps deceptive? *Journal of Mammalogy* 75: 692-699.

O'Farrell, M.J., Kaufman, D.W. & Lundahi, D.W. (1977) Use of live-trapping with the assessment line method for density estimation. *Journal of Mammalogy* 58: 575-582.

Ohgushi, R. (1986) Difference in effeciency of four types of rodent traps. *Applied Entomology and Zoology* 21: 627-629.

Oksanen, L., Fretwell, S.D. and Jarvinen, O. (1979) Interspecific aggression and the limiting similarity of close competitors: the problem of size gaps in some community arrays. *American Naturalist* 114: 117-129.

Olmos, F., Galetti, M., Paschoal, M. & Mendes, S.L. (1993) Habits of the southern Bamboo rat, *Kannabateomys amblyonyx* (Rodentia, Echimyidae) in southeastern Brazil. *Mammalia* 57: 325-333.

O'Reilly, H.M., Mansergh, I. & Willie, R. (1986) Daily pattern of activity of a captive mountain pygmy-possum, *Burramys parvus* (Broom) (Marsupialia: Burramyidae). *Australian Mammalogy* 9: 53-55.

Osawa, R. & Woodall, P.F.

(1990) Feeding strategies of the swamp wallaby, *Wallabia bicolor*, on North Island, Queensland. II: Effects of seasonal changes in diet quality on intestinal morphology. *Australian Wildlife Research* 17: 623-632.

(1992a) A comparative study of macroscopic and microscopic dimensions of the intestine in five Macropods (Marsupialia: Macropodidae). I. Allometric relationships. *Australian Journal of Zoology* 40: 91-98.

(1992b) A comparative study of macroscopic and microscopic dimensions of the intestine in five Macropods (Marsupialia: Macropodidae). II. Relationship with feeding habits and fibre content of the diet. *Australian Journal of Zoology* 40: 99-113.

Osbourne, W.S. & Preece, M.A. (1987) Extension of the range of the smoky mouse, *Pseudomys fumeus* (Rodentia: Muridae), into the Australian Capital territory. *Australian Mammalogy* 10: 35-36.

Ostfeld, R.S. & Heske, E.J. (1993) Sexual dimorphism and mating systems in voles. *Journal of Mammaolgy* 74: 230-233.

Ostfeld, R.S., Miller, M.C. & Schnurr, J. (1993) Ear tagging increased tick (*Ixodes dammini*) infestation rates of white-footed mice (*Peromyscus leucopus*). *Journal of Mammalogy* 74: 651-655.

Palanza, P., Parmigiani, S. & vom Saal, F.S. (1994) Male urinary cues stimulate intra-sexual aggression and urine-marking in wild female mice, *Mus musculus domesticus*. *Animal Behaviour* 48: 245-247.

Pankakoski, E. (1979) The influence of weather on the activity of the common shrew. *Acta Theriologica* 24: 522-526.

Payne, J.M. & Chamings, J.(1964) The anaesthesia of laboratory rodents. In Graham-Jones, O. (ed) *Small Mammal Anaesthesia*. pp 103-108. Pergamon Press, Oxford.

de Paz, O. (1986) Age estimation and post-natal growth of the greater mouse bat *Myotis myotis* (Borkhausen 1797) in Guadalajara, Spain. *Mammalia* 50: 243-251.

Pearson, D.J. & Robinson, A.C. (1990) New records of the sandhill dunnart, *Sminthopsis psammophila* (Marsupialia: Dasyuridae) in south and western Australia. *Australian Mammalogy* 13: 57-59.

Pelikan, J. (1989) Small mammals in fragments of *Robinia pseudacacia* stands. *Folia Zoologica* 38: 199-212.

Pennycuik, P.R. & Cowan, R. (1990) Odour and food preferences of house mice, *Mus musculus*. *Australian Journal of Zoology* 38: 241- 247.

Perrin, M.R. (1975) Trap deaths. *Acta Theriologica* 20: 167-174.

Perrin, M.R. & Curtis, B.A. (1980) Comparitive morphology of the digestive system of nineteen species of southern African myomorph rodents in relation to diet and evolution. *South African Journal of Zoology* 15: 22-33.

Pigozzi, G. (1988) Quill marking, a method to identify crested porcupine individually. *Acta Theriologica* 33: 138-142.

Du Plessis, A. & Kerley, G.I.H. (1991) Refuge strategies and habitat segregation in two sympatric rodents *Otomys unisulcatus* and *Parotomys brantsii*. *Journal of Zoology* (London) 224: 1-10.

Du Plessis, A., Kerley, G.H.I. & Deo Winter, P.E. (1992) Refuge microclimates of rodents: a surface nesting *Otomys unisulcatus* and a burrowing *Parotomys brantsii*. *Acta Theriologica* 37: 351-358.

Poole, T. (1994) Alternatives to `toe clipping' for identifying small vertebrates. *Association for the Study of Animal Behaviour Newsletter* 20: 7-8.

Price, M.V. (1978) The role of microhabitat in structuring desert rodent communities. *Ecology* 59: 910-921.

Price, M.V. (1982) Ecological consequences of body size: a model for patch choice in desert rodents. *Oecologia* 59: 384-392.

Price, M.V. & Brown, J.H. (1983) Patterns of morphology and resource use in North American desert rodent communities. *Great Basin Naturalist Memoirs* 7: 117-134.

Provensal, M.C. & Polop, J. (1993) Growth and determination of age in *Calomys musculinus* (Rodentia, Cricetidae). *Mammalia* 57: 244-254.

Pucek, Z. & Lowe, V.P.W. (1975) Age criteria in small mammals. *International Biological Programme* 5: 55-72.

Pucek, Z., Jedrzejewski, W., Jedrzejewska, B. & Pucek, M. (1993) Rodent population dynamics in a primeval deciduous forest (Bialowieza National Park) in relation to weather, seed crop, and predation. *Acta Theriologica* 38: 199-232.

Pugh, S.R., Ostfeld, R.S. & Tamarin, R.H. (1993) Reproductive asynchrony and its potential role in the mating system of meadow voles. *Acta Theriologica* 38: 263-271.

Putman, R.J.(1984) Facts from Faeces. *Mammal Review* 14: 79-97.

Quéré, par J.P., Giraudoux, P. Delattre, P. & Faivre, B. (1994) Détermination de la structure en âge relatif d'une population de *Microtus arvalis* (Rongeurs, Arvicolidés) par mesures ostéométriques crâniennes ou mandibulaires. *Mammalia* 58: 269-282.

Rana, B.D. (1986) Effect of trap placement on trapping success of small mammals. *Saugetierkundliche Mitteilungen* 32: 261-264.

Randolph, S.E. (1973) A tracking technique for comparing individual home ranges of small mammals. *Journal of Zoology* (London) 170: 509-520.

Rathbun, G.(1979) The social structure and ecology of elephant-shrews. *Advanced Ethology* 20: 1-76.

Read, D.G. (1988) Weather and trap response of the Dasyurid Marsupials *Smithopsis crassicaudata, Planigale gilesi* and *P. tenuirostris. Australian Wildlife Research* 15: 139-148.

Read, D.G. (1989) Microhabitat separation and diel activity patterns of *Planigale gilesi* and *P. tenuirostris* (Marsupialia: Dasyuridae). *Australian Mammalogy* 12: 45-53.

Read, V.T. (1987) Trap disturbance during the survey of small mammal communities. *Victorian Naturalist* 104: 150-153.

Reichman, O.J., Wicklow, D.T. & Rebar, C. (1985) Ecological and mycological characteristics of caches in the mounds of *Dipodomys spectabilis. Journal of Mammalogy* 66: 643-651.

Reynolds, P. & Gorman, M.L. (1994) Seasonal variation in the activity patterns of the Orkney vole *Microtus arvalis orcadensis. Journal of Zoology* (London) 233: 605-616.

Rice-Oxley, S.B. (1993) Caching behaviour of red squirrels *Sciurus vulgaris* under conditions of high food availability. *Mammal Review* 23: 93-100.

Richards, G.C. (1986) Predation on a platypus, *Ornithorhynchus anatinus* (Monotremata: Ornithorhynchidae), by a goshawk. *Australian Mammalogy* 9: 67.

Rickart, E. & Heaney, L. (1991) A new species of Chrotomys (Rodentia: Muridae) from Luzon Island, Philippines. *Proceedings of the Biological Society of Washington* 104: 387-398.

Robinette, W.L., Loveless, C.M. & Jones, D.A. (1974) Field tests of strip census methods. *Journal of Wildlife Management* 38: 81-96.

Robinson, F. (1989) Dental, palate and tongue imprints of bats: a new field technique. *Journal of Zoology* (London) 219: 681-684.

Robinson, G.R., Holt, R.D., Gaines, M.S., Hamburg, S.P., Johnson, M.L., Fitch, H.S. & Martinko, E.A. (1992) Diverse and contrasting effects of habitat fragmentation. *Science* 257: 524-526.

Rogovin, K.A. (1992) Habitat use by two species of Mongolian marmots (*Marmota sibirica* and *M. baibacina*) in a zone of sympatry. *Acta Theriologica* 37: 345-350.

Rogovin, K.A., Shenbrot, G.I., Surov, A.V. & Idris, M. (1994) Spatial organisation of a rodent community in the western Rajasthan desert (India). *Mammalia* 58: 243-260.

Rose, R.K., Slade, N.A. & Honacki, J.H. (1977) Live trap preference among grassland mammals. *Acta Theriologica* 22: 296-307.

Rosenberg, D.K. & Anthony, R.G. (1993) Differences in trapping mortality rates of northern flying squirrels. *Canadian Journal of Zoology* 71: 660-663.

Rosevear, D.R. (1969) *The Rodents of West Africa*. British Museum Natural History, London.

Rotenberry, J.T. & Wiens, J.A. (1980) Habitat structure, patchyness, and avian communities in North American steppe vegetation: a multivariate analysis. *Ecology* 61: 1228-1250.

Rowe, F.P. (1970) The response of wild house mice (*Mus musculus*) to live-traps marked with their own and by a foreign mouse odour. *Journal of Zoology* (London) 162: 517-520.

Sagara, N., Abe, H. & Okabe, H. (1993) The persistence of moles in nesting at the same site as indicated by mushroom fruiting and nest reconstruction. *Canadian Journal of Zoology* 71: 1690-1693.

Salamon, M. & Klettenheimer B, (1994) A new technique for marking and later recognising small mammals in the field *Journal of Zoology* (London) 233: 314-317.

Saltz, D. & Alkon, P.U. (1985) A simple computer-aided method for estimating radio-location error. *Journal of Wildlife Management* 49: 664-668.

Sanderson, G.C. & Sanderson, B.C. (1964) Radio-tracking rats in Malaya - a preliminary study. *Journal of Wildlife Management* 28: 752-768.

Scheffer, V.B.& Dalquest, W.W. (1942) A new shrew from Destruction island, Washington. *Journal of Mammalogy* 23: 333-335.

Schieck, J.O. & Millar, J.S. (1985) Alimentary tract measurements as indicators of diets of small mammals. *Mammalia* 49: 101-103.

Schipanov, N.A. (1987) Universal live trap for small mammals. *Zoologicheskii Zhurnal* 66: 759-761.

Schon, I. & Korn, H. (1992) Causes and magnitude of body weight changes in tra-confined bank voles, *Clethrionomys glareolus*. *Journal of Zoology* (London) 227: 319-322.

Schooley, R.L., van Horne, B. & Burnham, K.P. (1993) Passive integrated transponders for marking free-ranging Townsend's ground squirrels. *Journal of Mammalogy* 74: 480-484.

Schwan, T.G. (1986) Comparison of catches of two sizes of Sherman live traps in a grassland in Lake Nakuru National Park, Kenya. *African Journal of Ecology* 24: 31-35.

Scott, T.G. (1942) Ear tags on mice. *Journal of Mammalogy* 23: 339.

Scotts, D.J. & Craig, S.A. (1988) Improved hair-sampling tube for the detection of rare mammals. *Australian Wildlife Research* 15: 469-472.

Searle, J.B. (1985) Methods for determining the sex of common shrews (*Sorex araneus*). *Journal of Zoology* (London) 206: 279-282.

Seebeck, J.H., Suckling, G.C. & Macfarlane, M.A. (1983) Leadbeater's possum - survey by stagwatching. *Victorian Naturalist* 100: 92-97.

Sewell, G.D. (1968) Ultrasound in rodents. *Nature* 217: 682-683.

Sgardelis, S.P. & Margaris, N.S. (1992) Effects of fire on birds and rodents of a phryganic (east Mediterranean) ecosystem. *Israel Journal of Zoology* 38: 1-8.

Shadle, A.R. & Ploss, W.R. (1942) A metal restraining tube for animals. *Journal of Mammalogy* 23: 441-443.

Shaw, M.W. & Milner, C. (1967) The use of insulating covers for Longworth traps. *Journal of Zoology* (London) 153: 546-551.

Sherwin, W.B. (1991) Collecting mammalian tissue and data for genetic studies. *Mammal Review* 21: 21-30.

Shore, R.F. & Yalden, D.W. (1991) The effect of different lubricant oils on capture success in Longworth traps. *Journal of Zoology* (London) 225: 659-662.

Simonetti, J.A. (1986) On the assessment of trapping success. *Acta Theriologica* 31: 171-175.

Singleton, G.R. (1987) A comparison of the effectiveness of pitfall and longworth live trapping techniques in population studies of the house mouse. *Acta Theriologica* 32: 11-20.

Skalski, J.R. & Robson, D.S. (1992) *Techniques for Wildlife Investigations: design and analysis of capture data.* Academic Press, London.

Slade, N.A., Eifler, M.A. Gruenhagen, N.M. & Davelos, A.L. (1993) Differential effectiveness of standard and long Sherman livetraps in capturing small mammals. *Journal of Mammalogy* 74: 156-161.

Smales, L.R., Miller, A.K. & Obendorf, D.L. (1990) Parasites of the water rat, *Hydromys chrysogaster*, from Victoria and south Australia. *Australian Journal of Zoology* 37: 657-663.

Smith, C.C. (1978) Structure and function of the vocalizations of tree squirrels (*Tamiasciurus*). *Journal of Mammalogy* 59: 793-808.

Smith, P.A., Smith, J.A., Tattersall, F.H., Lancaster, V., Natynczuk, S.E. & Seymour, R.S. (1993) The ship rat (*Rattus rattus*) on Lundy, 1991. *Journal of Zoology* (London) 231: 689-695.

Smith, P.W., Borden, D.L. & Endres, K.M. (1994) Scent-station visits as an index to abundance of raccoons: an experimental manipulation. *Journal of Mammalogy* 75: 637-647.

Smith, A.P., Lindenmayer, D.B., Begg, R.J., Macfarlane, M.A., Seebeck, J.H. & Suckling, G.C. (1989) An evaluation of the stagwatching technique for census of possums and gliders in tall open forest. *Australian Wildlife Research* 16: 575-580.

Smolen, M.J., Pitts, R.M. & Bickham, J.W. (1993) A new subspecies of pocket gopher (*Geomys*) from texaz (Mammalia: Rodentia: Geomyidae). *Proceeding of the Biology Society of Washington* 106: 5-23.

Smythe, N. (1978) *The Natural History of the Central American Agouti (Dasyprocta punctata)*. Smithsonian Contributions to Zoology No. 257.

Snipes, R.L. & Kriete, A. (1991) Quantitative investigation of the area and volume in different compartments of the intestine of 18 mammalian species. *Z. Säugetierkunde* 56: 225-244.

Snyder, M.A. & Linhart, Y.B. (1994) Nest-site selection by Abert's squirrel: chemical characteristics of nest trees. *Journal of Mammalogy* 75: 136-141.

Soderquist, T.R. & Dickman, C.R. (1988) A technique for marking marsupial pouch young with flourescent pigment tatoos. *Australian Wildlife Research* 15: 561-563.

Soriguer, R.C. & Amat, J.A. (1980) On the structure and function of the burrows of the Mediterranean vole (*Pitymys duodecimcostatus*). *Acta Theriologica* 25: 268-270.

Southern, H.N. (1965) The trap-line index to small mammal populations. *Journal of Zoology* (London) 147: 217-221.

Southern, H.N. (1973) A yardstick for measuring populations of small rodents. *Mammal Review* 3: 1-10.

Springer, J.T. (1979) Some sources of bias and sampling error in radio triangulation. *Journal of Wildlife Management* 43: 926-935.

Stallings, J.R., Kierulff, M.C.M. & Silva, L.F.B.M. (1994) Use of space, and activity patterns of Brazilian Bamboo Rats (*Kannabateomys amblyonyx*) in exotic habitat. *Journal of Tropical Ecology* 10: 431-438.

Stapp, P., Young, J.K., Vandewoude, S. & van Horne, B. (1994) An evaluation of the pathological effects of flourescent powder on deer mice (*Peromyscus maniculatus*). *Journal of Mammalogy* 75: 704-709.

Steiner, K.E. (1981) Nectivory and potential pollination be a neotrapical marsupial. *Annals of the Missouri Botanical Garden* 68: 505-513.

Stephenson, P.J. (1994) Seasonality effects on small mammal trap success in Madagascar. *Journal of Tropical Ecology* 10: 439-444.

Stoddart, D.M (1970) Individual range, dispersion and dispersal in a population of water voles (*Arvicola terrestris* (L.)). *Journal of Animal Ecology* 39: 403-425.

Stirton, R.A. (1944) Tropical mammal trapping I. The water mouse *Rheomys*. *Journal of Mammalogy* 25: 337-343.

Stowe, L.G. & Wade, M.J. (1979) The detection of small-scale patterns in vegetation. *Journal of Ecology* 67: 1047-1064.

Suckling, G.C. (1978) A hair sampling tube for the detection of small mammals in trees. *Australian Wildlife Research* 5: 249-252.

Summerlin, C.T. & Wolfe, J.L. (1973) Social influences on trap response of the cotton rat, *Sigmodon hispidus*. *Communications in Behavioural Biology* 6: 105-109.

Swihart, R.K. & Slade, N.A. (1985) Testing for independence of observations in animal movement. *Ecology* 66: 1176-1184.

Tallmon, D. & Mills, L.S. (1994) Use of logs within home ranges of California red-backed voles on a remnant of forest. *Journal of Mammalogy* 75: 97-101.

Tamura, N. (1993) Role of sound communication in mating of Malaysian *Callosciurus* (Sciuridae). *Journal of Mammalogy* 74: 468-476.

Tamura, N. & Young, H.S. (1993) Vocalizations in response to predators in three species of Malaysian *Callosciurus* (Sciuridae). *Journal of Mammalogy* 74: 703-714.

Tattersall, F. & Whitbread, S. (1994) A trap-based comparison of the use of arboreal vegetation by populations of bank vole (*Clethrionomys glareolus*) woodmouse (*Apodemus sylvaticus*) and common dormouse (*Muscardinus avellanarius*). *Journal of Zoology* (London) 233: 309-314.

Taylor, K.D. (1973) A mechanical device for monitoring the movements of small mammals that use runways or shelters. *Journal of Zoology* (London) 171: 456-457.

Taylor, K. (1994) Mucking in together. *BBC Wildlife* 12 (Sept): 12.

Taylor, J.M., Calaby, J.H. & Smith, S.C. (1990) Reproduction in New Guinean *Rattus* and comparison with Australian *Rattus*. *Australian Journal of Zoology* 38: 587-602.

Tchernov, E. (1992) The Afro-Arabian component in the Levantine mammalian fauna - a short biogeographical review. *Israel Journal of Zoology* 38: 155-192.

Tedman, R.A. & Hall, L.S. (1985) The absorptive surface area of the small intestine of *Pteropus poliocephalus* (Megachiroptera: Pteropodidae): an important factor in rapid food transit? *Australian Mammalogy* 8: 271-278.

Teerink, B.J. (1991) *Hair of West-European mammals*. Cambridge University Press, Cambridge.

Tepper, E.E. (1967) *Statistical Methods in Using Mark-Recapture Data for Population Estimation*. US Deapartment of the Interior, Washington DC.

Teska, W.R. & Pinder, J.E. (1986) Effects of nutrition on age determination using eye lens weights. *Growth* 50: 362-370.

Tew, T. (1987) A comparison of small mammal responses to clean and dirty traps. *Journal of Zoology* (London) 212: 361-364.

Tew, T., Todd, I.A., & Macdonald, D.W. (1994a) Temporal changes in olfactory preferences in murid rodents revealed by live-trapping. *Journal of Mammalogy* 75: 750-756.

Tew, T.E., Todd, I.A. & Macdonald, D.W. (1994b) The effects of trap spacing on population estimation of small mammals. *Journal of Zoology* 233: 340-344.

Thompson, I.D. & Macauley, A.L. (1987) Comparative efficiency of new and old-style museum special traps in capturing small mammals. *Canadian Field Naturalist* 101: 608-610.

Timchenko, L.I. (1986) Automatic platform trap for decreasing the numbers of voles in forest plantations. *Zoologicheskii Zhurnal* 65: 1568-1570.

Timchenko, L.I. (1987) A trap of permenent action for rodents. *Zoologicheskii Zhurnal* 66: 762-764.

Twigg, G.I. (1975a) Catching mammals *Mammal Review* 5: 83-100.

Twigg, G.I. (1975b) Marking mammals. *Mammal Review* 5: 101-116.

Twigg, G.I. (1978) Marking mammals by tissue removal. In Stonehouse, B. (ed) *Animal Marking, recognition marking of animals in research*. pp. 109-118. Macmillan Press Ltd, London.

Ventura, J. (1992) Coats and moults in *Arvicola terrestris* from the northeast of the Iberian Peninsula. *Zoologische Abhandlungen, Staatliches Museum für Tierkunde Dresden* 47: 95-110.

Ventura, J. (1993) A discriminant function for sexual determination in *Arvicola terrestris monticola* (Rodentia, Arvicolidae) based on the morphology of the innominate bone. *Mammalia* 57: 435-440.

Vickery, W.L. & Bider, J.R. (1978) The effect of weather on *Sorex cinereus* activity. *Canadian Journal of Zoology* 56: 291-297.

Vickery, W.L. & Bider, J.R. (1981) The influence of weather on rodent activity. *Journal of Mammalogy* 62: 140-145.

Viitela, J.A. (1989) A method to estimate the survival differences among overwintered microtines: cyclic *Clethrionomys rufocanus* (Sund.) at Kilpisjarvi, Finnish Lapland. *Zeitschrift fur Saugetierkund* 54: 223-228.

de Villiers, M.S., van Aarde, R.J. & Dot, H.M. (1994) Habitat utilization by the Cape porcupine *Hystrix afircaeaustralis* in a savanna ecosystem. *Journal of Zoology* (London) 323: 539-549.

Vose, H. (1973) Feeding habits of the western Australian honey possum, *Tarsipes spenserae*. *Journal of Mammalogy* 54: 245-247.

Walker, P.L. & Cant, J.G.H. (1977) A population survey of Kinkajous (*Potos flavus*) in a seasonally dry tropical forest. *Journal of Mammalogy* 58: 100-102.

Wallis, R.L. & Brunner, H. (1987) Changes in mammalian prey of foxes, *Vulpes vulpes* (Carnivora: Vanidae) over 12 years in a forest park near Melbourne, Victoria. *Australian Mammalogy* 10: 43-44.

Weisel, S. & Brandl, R. (1993) The small mammal fauna in a hedge of north-eastern Bavaria. *Z. Säugetierkunde* 58: 368-375.

Wells, M.D., Taylor, W.A., Tedd, J.R., Long, E., Palmer, G. & Grant, I. (1994) *Preliminary Field Report of the University of Aberdeen Project Madagascar 1994*. Unpublished report of the University of Aberdeen Project Madagascar.

West, S.D. (1985) Differential capture between old and new models of the museum special snap trap. *Journal of Mammalogy* 66: 798-800.

White, G.C. & Garrott, R.A. (1986) Effects of biotelemetry triangulation error on detecting habitat selection. *Journal of Wildlife Management* 50: 509-513.

White, G.C. & Garrott, R.A. (1990) *Analysis of Wildlife Radio-Tracking Data*. Academic Press, Inc., San Diego.

Whiteside, G.H., Oates, J.F., Green, S.M. & Kluberdanz, R.P. (1988) Estimating primate densities from transects in a west African rain forest: a compariopsn of techniques. *Journal of Animal Ecology* 57: 345-367.

Wiener, J.G. & Smith, M.H. (1972) Relative efficiencies of four small mammal traps. *Journal of Mammalogy* 53: 868-873.

Wiens, D., Renfree, M. & Woler, R.O. (1979) Pollen loads of honey possums (*Tarsipes spenserae*) and non-flying mammal pollination in southwestern Australia. *Annals of the Missouri Botanical Garden* 66: 830-838.

Wiens, D. & Rourke, J.P. (1978) Rodent pollination in southern African Protea spp. *Nature* 276: 71-73.

Wiens, D., Rourke, J.P., Caspar, B.B., Rickart, E.A., LaPine, T.R., Peterson, C.J. & Channing, A. (1983) Non-flying mammal pollination of southern African proteas: a non-coevolved system. *Annals of the Missouri Botanical Garden* 70: 1-31.

Williams, O. (1962) A technique for studying microtine food habits. *Journal of Mammalogy* 43: 365-368.

Williams, S. (1979) *A Guide to the Literature Concerning the Management of Recent Mammal Collections.* Texas Tech University, Museology Publications No. 5.

Willan, K. (1979) Design and field tests of a modified small mammal livetrap. *South African Journal of Zoology*. 14: 81-84.

Willan, K. (1986a) Trap selection by some southern African small mammals. *South African Journal of Wildlife Research* 16: 53-57.

Willan, K. (1986b) Bait selection in laminate-toothed rats and other southern African small mammals. *Acta Theriologica* 31: 359-363.

Williams, D.F. & Braun, S.E. (1983) Comparison of pitfall and conventional traps for sampling small mammal populations. *Journal of Wildlife Management* 47: 841-845.

Wilson, D.E. & Reeder, D.M. (1993) *Mammal species of the World. A taxonomic and geographic reference.* Smithsonian Institution Press in association with American Society of Mammalogists, Washington.

Wilson, E.O. (1987) The arboreal ant fauna of the Peruvian Amazon forests: a first assessment. *Biotropica* 19: 245-251.

Winser, S. (1992) Writing expedition reports. In Winser, S. & McWilliam, N. (eds) *Expedition Planners' Handbook & Directory 1993-94.* pp360-367. Expedition Advisory Centre, London.

Witt, J.W. (1991) Fluctuations in the weight and trap response for *Glaucomys sabrinus* in western Oregon. *Journal of Mammalogy* 72: 612-615.

Wójcik, J.M. (1993) Chromosome races of the common shrew *Sorex araneus* in Poland: a model of karyotype evolution. *Acta Theriologica* 38: 315-338.

Wolff, J.O. (1993) Does the "Chitty Effect" occur in *Peromyscus. Journal of Mammalogy* 74: 846-851.

Wolff, J.O., Freeberg, M.H. & Dueser, R.D. (1983) Interspecific territoriality in two sympatric species of *Peromyscus* (Rodentia: Cricetidae). *Behavioral Ecology and Sociobiology* 12: 237-242.

Wolton, R.J. (1985) The ranging and nesting behaviour of Wood mice, *Apodemus sylvaticus* (Rodentia: Muridae), as revealed by radio-tracking. *Journal of Zoology* (London) 206: 203-224.

Wolton, R.J. (1985) A possible role for faeces in rang-marking by the wood mouse, *Apodemus sylvaticus*. *Journal of Zoology* (London) 206: 286-291.

Wood, D.H. (1988) Estimating rabbit density by counting dung pellets. *Australian Wildlife Research* 15: 665-671.

Woods, J.A. & Mead-Briggs, A.R. (1978) The daily cycle of activity in the mole (*Talpa europaea*) and its seasonal changes, as revealed by radioactive monitoring of the nest. *Journal of Zoology* (London) 184: 563-572.

Woodall, P.F. (1989) Habitat of *Melomys cervinipes* (Rodentia: Muridae) on Carlisle Island, central Queensland. *Australian Mammalogy* 12: 31-32.

Woodall, P.F. (1993) Dispersion and habitat preference of the water vole (*Arvicola terrestris*) on the river Thames. *Z. Säugetierkunde* 58: 160-171.

Yalden, D.W. & Morris (1990) *The Analysis of Owl Pellets*. Occasional Publications of the Mammal Society no. 13. The Mammal Society, Bristol.

Ylönen, H. (1990) Spatial avoidance between the bank vole *Clethrionomys glareolus* and the harvest mouse *Micromys minutus*: an experimental study. *Annals Zoologici Fennici* 27: 313-320.

Yom-Tov, Y. (1993) Size variation in *Rhabdomys pumilio*: a case of character release? *Z. Säugetierkunde* 58: 48-53.

Zanchin, N.I.T., Sbalqueiro, I.J., Langguth, A., Bossle, R.C., Castro, E.C., Oliveira, L.F.B. & Mattevi, M.S. (1992) Karyotype and species diversity of the genus *Delomys* (Rodentia, Cricetidae) in Brazil. *Acta Theriologica* 37: 163-169.

Zhu, S. (1985) The annual changes of mean body weight and capture rates of seven rodents in northern Xinjiaqng, China, for ten years. In Kawamichi, T. (ed) *Contempory Mammalogy in China and Japan*. pp. 73-77. Mammalogical Society of Japan.

Ziegler, A.C. (1984) A Papua New Guinea specimen of *Hydromys hussoni* Musser and Piik, 1982 (Rodentia: Muridae). *Australian Mammalogy* 7: 101-105.

Zubaid, A. & Gorman, M.L. (1991) The diet of woodmice, *Apodemus sylvaticus*, living in a sand dune habitat in North-east Scotland. *Journal of Zoology* (London) 225: 227-232.

Zuk, M. & Decruyenaere, J.G. (1994) Measuring individual variation in colour: a comparison of two techniques. *Biological Journal of the Linnean Society* 53: 165-173.

Section Fifteen
RECOMMENDED READING

(Including the best books on Continent-by-Continent and Country basis)

General

Note: this list is not intended to be exhaustive or all inclusive. Not all the books listed are of the same scientific quality. The publications will provide a general guide - specific revisions should be sought and consulted for up to date taxonomy (if in doubt, use Wilson & Reeder [1993] or Honacki *et al.*, [1982].

Wilson, D.E. & Reeder, D.M. (1993) *Mammal species of the World. A taxonomic and geographic reference.* Smithsonian Institution Press in association with American Society of Mammalogists, Washington. (The fount of all taxonomic wisdom - uses a classification generally accepted by almost all small mammal workers. Very useful for working out synonomies, though check more recent literature for any further revisions).

Honacki, J.H., Kinman, K.E. & Koeppl, J.W. (1982) *Mammal Species of the World: A Taxonomic and Geographical Reference.* Allan Press & Association of Systematists, Collins. (Replaced by Wilson & Reeder [above] but still a valuable reference in its own right).

Mammalian Species. (A very useful occassional publication. Provides literature summaries and biological overviews for selected species).

Nowak, R.M. (1991) *Walker's Mammals of the World.* John Hopkins University Press. 2 vols. (Covers every single known mammal in the world up to 1991 - check for taxonomic revisions in later literature).

Recent Literature of Mammalogy. Occasional supplement to *Journal of Mammalogy*, from 1970 to present. Organized by subject and geographical area.

Sims, R.W. (ed.) (1980) *Animal Identification - a reference guide.* Volume 2: Land and Freshwater Animals (not insects). BMNH & John Wiley & Sons, Chichester. (This is a check list of check lists; done by taxonomic group and geographical region)

Asia

General

Cranbrook, Earl of (1992) *Mammals of South-East Asia*. Oxford University Press, Oxford.

Borneo

Medway, G. (The Earl of Cranbrook) (1977) *Mammals of Borneo*. Monograph of the Malaysian Branch of the Royal Asiatic Society.

Payne, J., Francis, C.M. & Phillips, K. (1985) *A Field Guide to the Mammals of Borneo*. The Sabah Society and WWF-Malaysia

India

Mumford, R.E. & Whitaker, O. (1982) *Mammals of India*. Bloomington Indiana University Press.

Parrack, D.W. (ed.) (1966) *Indian Rodent Symposium*. John Hopkins University Press.

Prater, S.H. (1971) *The Book of Indian Mammals*. Bombay Natural History Society.

Indonesia

van der Zon, A.M.P. (1979) *Mammals of Indonesia*. FAO, Bogor.

Malaysia

Medway, G. (The Earl of Cranbrook) (1978) *Wild Mammals of Malaysia*. Oxford University Press.

Pakistan

Roberts, T.J. (1977) *The Mammals of Pakistan*. Ernest Benn Ltd, London.

Siddiqi, M.S. (1961) *Checklist of the mammals of Pakistan*, with particular reference to the mammal collection in the British Museum (Natural History), London. *Biologia* 7: 93-225.

Philippines

Alcasid, G.L. (1970) *Checklist of Philippine Mammals*. National Museum, Manilla.

Taylor, E.H. (1934) *Philippine Land Mammals*. Manilla.

Sri Lanka

Phillips, W.W.A. (1980) *Manual of the Mammals of Sri Lanka* (part II). Wildlife and Nature Protection Society of Sri Lanka.

Thailand

Lekagal, B., & McNeely J.A. (1988) *Mammals of Thailand*. Sahra Karn Bhact Co., Thailand.

Vietnam

van Peenen, P.F.D., Ryan, P.F. & Light, R.H. (1969) *Preliminary Identification Manual for Mammals of South Vietnam*. Smithsonian Institution, Washington.

Africa

West

Happold, D.C.D. (1987) *The Mammals of Nigeria*. Clarendon Press-Oxford University Press, Oxford.

Rosevear, D.R. (1969) *Rodents of West Africa*. British Museum Natural History, London.

East

Ansell, W.F.H. (1978) *The Mammals of Zambia*. Natural Parks and Wildlife Service, Chilanga.

Ansell, W.F.H. & Dowsett, R.J. (1988) *The Mammals of Malawi, an annotated check list and atlas*. Trendrine Press, Zennor.

Delany, M.J. (1974) *Rodents of Uganda*. British Museum (Natural History), London.

Kingdon, J. (1974) *East African Mammals; an atlas of evolution in Africa*. Volume IIa, Insectivores and Bats. Academic Press, London.

Kingdon, J. (1974b) *The Mammals of East Africa; an atlas of evolution in Africa*. Volume IIb, Lagomorphs and Rodents. Academic Press, London.

Smithers, R.H.N. (1968) *Check List and Atlas of the Mammals of Botswana*. National Museum of Rhodesia.

Smithers, R.H.N. (1971) *The Mammals of Botswana*. National Museum of Rhodesia.

South

Meester, J.A.J., Rautenbach, I.L., Dippenaar, N.J. & Becker, C.M. (1986) *Classification of Southern African Mammals*. Transvaal Museum Monograph No. 5.

Skinner J.D. & Smithers R.H.N. (1990) *The Mammals of the Southern African Sub-region*. University of Pretoria, Pretoria.

Stuart, C. & Stuart, T. (1988) *A Field Guide to the Mammals of Southern Africa*. New Holland, London.

North

Harrison, D.L. (1972) *Mammals of Arabia*, Volume III (Lagomorphs and Rodentia). Ernest Benn Ltd. London.

Harrison, D.L. & Bates, P.J.J. (1991) *The Mammals of Arabia*. Harrison Zoological Museum, Kent.

Osborn, D.J. & Helmy I. (1980) *The Mammals of Egypt*. Fieldiana (Zoology), ns, No. 5: 1-579.

The Americas

General

Cabrera, A. & Yepes, J. (1940) *Mamiferos Sud-Americanos (Vida Costumbres y Description)*. Compania Argentina de Editores, Buenos Aires.

Cabrera, A. (1960) *Catologo de los Mamiferos de America del Sur*. Vol. 2. Sirenia-Perissodactyla-Artiodactyla-Lagomorpha-Rodentia-Cetacea. Revista Museo Argentino de Ciencias Naturales 'Bernadino Rivadavia', Zoologia 4 (1-2):309-732.

Eisenberg, J.F. (1989) *Mammals of the Neotropics*, Volume One - The Northern Neotropics; Panama, Venezuela, Guyana, Suriname, French Guiana. Chicago University Press. Chicago.

Eisenberg, J.F. (1990) Neotropical Mammal *Communities*. In Gentry, A.H. (ed.) *Four Neotropical Forests*. pp. 358-370. Yale University Press.

Eisenberg, J.F. (ed.) (1979) *Vertebrate Ecology in the Northern Neotropics*. Smithsonian Institution Press, Washington DC.

Emmons, L.H. (1990) *Neotropical Rainforest Mammals - a Field Guide*. Chicago University Press.

Mares, M.A. & Genoways, H.H. (eds.) (1981) *Mammalian Biology in South America*. Special Publication Series, Pymatuning Laboratory, University of Pittsberg, Volume Six.

Patterson, B.D. & Timm, R.M. (eds.). (1987) *Studies in Neotropical Mammalogy*. Fieldiana (Zoology), ns, No. 39.

Redford, K.H. & Eisenberg, J.F. (eds.) (1989) *Advances in Neotropical Mammalogy*. Sandhill Crane Press, Gainesville, FLA.

North America

Alvares del Toro, M. (1977) Los Mamiferos de Chiapas. Universidad Autonomia de Chiapas, Tuxtla Gutierrez, Chiapas.

Hall, E.R. (1981) *Mammals of North America*. (2 Volumes). Wiley-Interscience Publications, John Wiley, New York.

Hamilton, W.J. & Whitaker, J.O. (1979) *Mammals of the Eastern United States*. Comstock Publishing, Ithaca.

Ingles, L.G. (1965) *Mammals of the Pacific States*. Stanford University Press.

Zeveloff, S.I. & Collett, F.R. (1988) *Mammals of the Intermontane West*. University of Utah Press, Salt Lake City.

Plus many mammal books on a state-by-state basis.

Central America

Alvares del Toro, M. (1977) *Los Mamiferos de Chiapas*. Universidad Autonomia de Chiapas, Tuxtla Gutierrez, Chiapas.

Aranda, J.M. (1981) *Rastos de los mamiferos silvestres de Mexico*. Instituto Nacional de Investigaciones sobre Recursos Bioticos.

Bart, W.H. & Stirton (1961) *Mammals of El Salvador*. Miscellaneous Publications of the Museum of Zoology, University of Michigan, No. 117.

Glanz, W.E. (1990) Neotropical mammal densities: how unusual is the community on Barro Colorado Island, Panama? In Gentry, A.H. (ed.) *Four Neotropical Forests*. pp. 287-313. Yale University Press.

Goodwin, G.G. (1969) Mammals fron the State of Oaxaca, Mexico, in the American Museum of Natural History. *Bulletin of the American Museum of Natural History* 141: 1-269.

Ibarra, J.A. (1959) *Mamiferos de Guatamala*. Ediciones Ministerio de Educacion.

Janzen, D.H. (ed.). (1983) *Costa Rican Natural History*. Chicago University Press, Chicago.

Mora, J.M. & Moeira, I. (1984) *Mamiferos de Costa Rica*. Editorial Universidad Estatal Distancia, San Jose.

Ramirez-Palida, J., Wilchris R.L., Mudespacher, C. & Lira, I. (1982) *Catologo de los Mamiferos Terrestres Naturais de Mexico*. Universidad Autonomo Metropolitana.

Ramirez-Palida. J., Britton, M.C., Perdomo, A. & Castro, A. (1986) *Guia de los Mamiferos de Mexico - referencias hasta 1983*. Universidad Autonomo Metropolitana.

Wilson, D.E. (1990) Mammals of La Selva. In Gentry, A.H. (ed.) *Four Neotropical Forests*. pp. 273-286. Yale University Press.

South America

Eisenberg, J.F. & Redford, K.H.. (1979) A biogeographic analysis of the mammalian fauna of Venezuela. In Eisenberg, J.F. (ed.) *Vertebrate Ecology in the Northern Neotropics*. pp. 31-36. Smithsonian Institute, Washington DC.

Glade, A.A. (ed.) (1987) *Red List of Chilean Terrestrial Vertebrates*. Santiago, Chile.

Husson, A.M. (1978) *The Mammals of Suriname*. Zoologische Monographieen van het Rijksmuseum van Natuuraijke Historie No. 2. Leiden.

Janson, C.H. & Emmons, L.H. (1990) Ecological structure of the non-flying mammal community at Cocha Cashu Biological Station, Manu National Park, Peru. In Gentry, A.H. (ed) *Four Neotropical Forests*. pp. 314-338. Yale University Press.

Malcolm, J.R. (1990) Estimation of mammalian densities in continious forest north of Manaus (Brazil).In Gentry, A.H. (ed.) *Four Neotropical Forests*. pp. 339-357. Yale University Press.

Mares, M.A., Ojeda, R.A. & Barquez, R.M. (1989) *Guide to the Mammals of Salta Province, Argentina*. University of Oklahoma Press.

Olrog, C.C. & Lucero, M.M. (1981) *Guia de los Mamiferos Argentinos*. Ministerio de Cultura y Educacion, Tucuman.

Peterson, N.E. and Pine, R.H. (1982) Chave para identificacao de mamiferos da regiao amazonica brasilera com execao dos quiropteros e primatas. *Acta Amazonica* 12: 465-482.

Pine, R.H. (1973) Mammals (exclusive of bats) of Belem, Para, Brazil. *Acta Amazonica* 3: separate.

Australasia

Strahan, R. (ed.) (1983) *The Complete Book of Australian Mammals*. The Australian Museum, Sydney.

Tate, G.H.H. (1951) Rodents of Australia and New Guinea. *Bulletin of the American Museum of Natural History* 97: 187-430.

Walton, D.W. & Richardson, B.J. (eds) (1989) *The Fauna of Australia - Volume 1 Mammalia*. Australian Government Publishing Service, Sydney.

Cover illustration

From *In the Australian Bush* by Richard Semon, pub. 1899 by MacMillan, London (page 167)